THE BICYCLE PLANNING BOOK

The Bicycle Planning Book

Mike Hudson

Open Books/Friends of the Earth

First published in 1978 by Open Books Publishing Ltd, 11 Goodwin's Court, London WC2N 4LB and by Friends of the Earth, 9 Poland Street, London W1V 3DG

© Mike Hudson 1978

ISBN 0 7291 0172 X

This book is printed on recycled paper.

British Library Cataloguing in Publication Data

Hudson, Mike
  The bicycle planning book
  1. Cycling — paths — Great Britain 2. Cycling — Great Britain
  3. Urban transportation policy — Great Britain
  I. Title II. Friends of the Earth
  388.4'1   HE363.G73C/   78-316552

  ISBN 0-7291-0172-X

Filmset in 9 on 11 point Linotron Imprint
Printed in Great Britain by
T. & A. Constable Ltd, Edinburgh

FRIENDS OF THE EARTH is an environmental pressure group funded by voluntary contributions. It has over 170 local groups in Britain and is part of a world-wide federation of similar organisations. FOE actively pursues campaigns on energy strategy, transport policy, the use of land, the protection of endangered species and the use of material resources. FOE is associated with the environmental research charity Earth Resources Research.

We are funded by the sale of publications and by voluntary contributions. If you would like to join Friends of the Earth or send a donation towards our campaign for the provision of cycling facilities or if you would like to receive a copy of our publications list or further information about our work please write to: Friends of the Earth, 9 Poland Street, London W1V 3DG (Tel: 01-434 1684).

Acknowledgements

I would like to thank the following individuals and organisations, without whose help this book could not have been produced: Tom Burke, Eric Claxton, Trevor Field, Jean Fraser, Elsa Gilbert, Clair Kirby, The London Borough of Sutton, Richard Macrory, Richard Matthews, David Pedley, and Gavin Smith.

The Department of Transport signs are reproduced with the permission of Her Majesty's Stationery Office. Diagrams are by Illustra Design Ltd.

I am particularly grateful to the four other members of the FOE Bicycle Planning Team for their contributions to this book. Finally, heartfelt thanks go to Mark Budden with whom I spent many hours editing various drafts and to Di Bell, my wife, for her never ending patience and encouragement.

Mike Hudson
December 1977

Biographical notes

This report is the result of a project set up by Friends of the Earth to look at cycling facilities. Over the past twelve months a team of five people have been working on the project:

Richard Brown is an honours engineering graduate from Cambridge, who recently completed an MPhil in Town Planning at London University. He has worked as a Transportation Planner and with the Kensington Bicycle Company. He is currently working with British Rail and is the organiser of the West London Bicycles Campaign.

Mike Hudson is an honours graduate in Engineering and Management. He is the co-author of THE SCHMALTS REPORT, a critique of transport planning in Merseyside, THE GREAT HEAT ESCAPE, a report about home insulation, and a project pack explaining how to campaign for improved home insulation. He used to work with British Rail and is currently Bicycles Campaigner for Friends of the Earth.

Dick Jones is an honours graduate in Geology and Geography. He has a diploma in Town Planning and is currently a Senior Planning Officer with the Greater London Council. He is also a company director of Friends of the Earth.

Nick Lester is an honours graduate in Architecture, Planning and Building. He has a diploma in Architecture from London University, has worked in local government and currently works with Transport 2000. He is coordinator of Lambeth FOE and the Lambeth Campaign for Cycling Safety.

Peter Trevelyan has an honours degree in Natural Sciences, an MSc in Transportation, and a diploma in Town Planning. He is a member of the Institute of Highway Engineers, the Royal Town Planning Institute and the Chartered Institute of Transport. He has worked in the Planning Department of a London Borough and is currently working as a transportation consultant. He is an active member of All Change to Bikes Westminster, Secretary of Central London Cyclists' Touring Club, and has organised the first educational course on bicycle planning in the UK.

Finally, the most important qualification of all, every member of the team is a regular cyclist.

Contents

Introduction

This report aims to fill a gap in the available literature about bicycles.[1] The arguments for encouraging planners to make provision for cyclists were set out in 'Give Way', a report published by FOE in 1974.[2] Since then, public interest in cycling has been growing fast, and the need for a document which could be used to encourage the implementation of networks of cycling facilities has become pressing. This report has two functions therefore. First of all, it sets out the arguments in favour of planning for the bicycle, and secondly, it gives a detailed description of a range of existing and proposed cycling facilities which will enable planners and engineers to select the most suitable designs for use in their particular area.

Recent increases in the price of oil and the realisation that demand for energy from fossil fuels will soon outstrip supply have made people more aware of a potential role for the bicycle in the future. In addition, the escalating costs of travelling by public transport will encourage many people to turn to the bicycle as a cheap and efficient means of door to door travel. Furthermore, increasing awareness of the quality of life, and in particular of the damage caused to the environment by the motor car, is causing a change in attitude towards our whole transport system. However, whilst these factors are working to persuade people to cycle, planners and engineers continue to provide for cars, at the expense and to the detriment of cyclists.

Our basic contention in this report is that if facilities to increase cyclists' safety are provided, more people will travel by bicycle. To divert a small proportion of the money spent on roads towards special cycling facilities would persuade many people who are at present put off by the unpleasantness and danger of mixing with motorised traffic to travel by bicycle.

[1] Technically the term bicycle refers to a machine which has two wheels – a cycle has any number of wheels. For simplicity we have consistently used the term bicycle, but the book is equally applicable to other types of cycle.
[2] Out of print.

In the first three chapters of this report we discuss the arguments for stimulating the provision of bicycle facilities in this country. Chapter four describes how the law affects the use of, and planning for, the bicycle. Chapters five and six describe cycle schemes in operation both in this country and abroad. In the final chapter, we aim to provide a comprehensive breakdown of the various types of facilities which can be provided to encourage the development of safe cycling.

We have concentrated our efforts on urban areas, since it is here that there is the greatest potential for cycling. We have not given detailed consideration to recreational or rural cycling facilities, although some of the ideas presented may be relevant to these situations.

An imaginative approach will be required to fit cycle route networks into the existing urban fabric. We have, therefore, only given broad guidelines within which the versatility of the bicycle can be fully exploited.

We would like our report to initiate a range of new and interesting approaches to bicycle planning and would therefore welcome feedback on the ideas in this report and on other new ideas which are developed. A positive approach to planning, involving close cooperation between environmentalists, cyclists, planners and engineers is surely the most appropriate way of providing facilities for cyclists and encouraging a means of transport which could have a great future.

1/Background

1.1 Historical context

For a million years man's own two feet have provided him with the transport means he required to satisfy his daily needs. It was only three thousand years ago that he began to ride on horseback or in horsedrawn carriages and these were the only means of transport until the beginning of the nineteenth century. Personal travel by horse-drawn transport was itself the monopoly of the social elite and the military right through until the time of the industrial revolution. Virtually all other journeys over land were made by foot.

With the advent of the industrial revolution, the developing industries required the support of an increasingly reliable and swift transport system, capable of carrying large loads of heavy and bulky material. For a time the canals, which were developed to satisfy this need, achieved their end with great success; but this particular form of transport was altogether unsuitable for providing greater personal mobility. With the rise of the railways, personal transport around the country became a realistic possibility, and the railways expanded swiftly. There remained however the problem of transport from railway stations to more inaccessible places.

It was into this picture that the bicycle made its first tentative appearances. From the first hobby-horse (1818) and the first velocipede (1863) the development of the bicycle was somewhat erratic. The vogue for 'Ordinaries', or penny farthings as we know them, distracted attention for a decade or two from the development of the 'safety bicycle', the true forerunner of the modern bicycle. The first of these was produced in 1873; in 1888 the pneumatic tyre was patented, and in 1890 Humber produced a diamond frame safety bicycle incorporating most of the features of the modern bicycle. Further developments have essentially been modifications of that design, with improved materials, braking systems and large-scale production techniques.

As the bicycle became increasingly popular, it offered the opportunity for many to share the roads previously only used by the carriages of the rich and the feet of the poor. It represented a distinct improvement over travel by foot in terms of speed and mobility. The bicycle was used to get to work, which might have been at most a few miles away, or into the nearest towns. By the end of the First World War bicycle design had been more or less standardised, and bicycle production hit new heights. The interwar years were the heyday of cycling, with many people owning bicycles, and most of these cycling regularly.

Back in 1899 the first motor cars made their appearance, and eyes began to turn away from the bicycle to this new and supposedly wonderful piece of machinery. It quickly became obvious that the car would be fast and bulky, capable of inflicting severe injury to anyone who strayed into its path. The development of road networks, systems to control motor vehicles, and areas to park them, all presented engineers, and more recently town planners, with challenges of unprecedented magnitude. The very advantages of the bicycle as a means of transport were among the factors which contributed to its decline. The bicycle was cheap, and hence readily available to a large proportion of the community, it was already modified to a form in which it provided a satisfactory means of transport for work, for sport and for leisure, and it required no new developments in the road system for its continued use. Because no particular problems were presented by planning for the bicycle, it tended to be forgotten and planning was geared to designing road systems and to controlling the motor car. This signalled the start of the decline of cycling.

The development of faster and cheaper cars encouraged the construction of road systems designed to allow them to travel at speed and unhindered by obstructions. The meanderings of cyclists and pedestrians had to be controlled and primitive forms of segregation were devised, developing gradually into the elaborate systems of herding, guardrailing, traffic lights and control systems in use today. Pedestrians walking in front of cars and cyclists sharing roads with cars ran an increasing risk of being injured in accidents.

Car production rose swiftly, and with increasing familiarity with the possibilities of travel by car, the popular perspective of distance altered. People began to see that with a car they would be able to make journeys that had previously seemed inconceivable. The time when each adult would possess his own car became a real possibility which people strove for. People who owned cars used them to find alternative or better paid work in more distant towns, and young people increasingly travelled to other parts of the country in search of work.

With the end of petrol rationing in 1952, these developments continued to accelerate. Motorised road transport opened up new possibilities for the transport of the materials of an industrial economy and during the 1960s planners and engineers increasingly assumed the general availability of private and public motor transport when designing new housing developments to replace slum housing and to cater for a growing population. The planning of land-use patterns began to follow the technique of 'zoning' geographical areas by function, so that housing estates, shopping areas and industrial estates became separated from each other, and roads suitable for the motor car connected these areas. The result of this is that we are now dependent for our food, our building materials and our life support systems on elaborate supply chains in which road transport plays an essential part.

However, more recently, the principles on which our towns and cities have been built have begun to be questioned. It is possible to design modifications to an existing urban fabric which favour the pedestrian and the cyclist. This is achieved by planning for nucleated settlements in which homes, workplaces, shops and recreational facilities will all be within a short distance of each other. People need access to these facilities and if they are all available within a small area, elaborate transport systems are no longer required. In addition, a more nucleated settlement pattern would encourage community spirit, community responsibility and personal independence from the remote systems on which we are dependent for our basic needs.

The general structure of our transport system is determined by our attitude to wide ranging socio-economic issues. We cannot be sure that the road systems we are providing today will be suitable for the type of society we will have in fifty or a hundred years' time. People are becoming increasingly aware of the finite limitations of our material resources. Transport and land-use patterns which encourage only limited consumption of these resources are likely to become both necessary and popular.

It is in this context that the future of the bicycle must be considered. The recent upsurge of interest in cycling and the increasing problems associated with road and rail networks are indications that bicycles might play a major role in our future transport systems.

In the 1960s universal car ownership and a permanently growing industrial economy were seen as realisable ideals. We now live in a period of austerity, but it is an austerity which challenges us to look forward. We have, as no generation before us has had, the tools with which to seize the opportunities to mould the future. It is a future in which the bicycle could play an important part.

1.2 The advantages of the bicycle

The bicycle is a simple piece of machinery, which everyone can understand, almost anyone can learn to ride, and most people can afford to buy and run.[1] No other means of transport combines this intrinsic simplicity and availability to the whole community. Thus the bicycle can rightly be called the most equitable means of transport which man has designed.

For certain groups of people, such as the under sixteens, the very poor and the elderly (who are not necessarily incapable of cycling), the bicycle may be the only means of transport which is available, particularly in urban areas where transport provision may appear to be good but is not readily available to them for practical or financial reasons.

In times of impending energy shortage, a machine which offers 1600 miles for the energy equivalent of a gallon of petrol demands to be given serious attention.[2] Similarly, the energy needed to manufacture just one car could be used to produce between 70 and 100 bicycles.

The bicycle is also a fast means of urban transport. Door to door journey times are not complicated by walking to and from car parks, bus stops or railway stations (Fig. 1.1). Traffic congestion affects a cyclist's speed less than it affects motorists. Most journeys to work are

[1] A working secondhand bicycle can be purchased for £20 and an excellent five speed touring bicycle for £50-£100. £15 per annum should be ample to cover running costs.

[2] *All Change*, No. 5. An alternative calculation comes from *New Scientist*, 8/10/75. A cyclist uses 23 kilocalories of energy per passenger mile whereas a car uses 630 kcal/passenger mile.

well within the range of the average cyclist, and for journeys under four miles in urban areas, cycling is faster than walking or travel by car, taxi, train, tube or bus.

The bicycle makes only small demands on valuable urban space. Bicycle storage space simply does not rank in the same class as garaging and fifteen cycles can be parked in one car parking space.

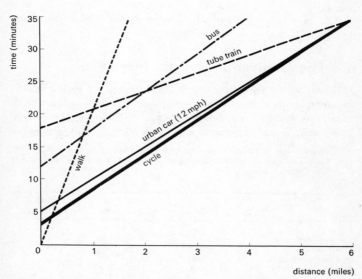

Figure 1.1 Door to door travel times by different means of transport.[3]

The bicycle also takes up little space when moving; a two way 12 ft wide cycleway caters for five times the traffic of a 24 ft wide road.[4] In the words of one engineer, bicycle planning gives people 'motorways for the price of footpaths'.[5] The private motor car, which accounts for only 11 per cent of all journeys to work in Central London, takes up 85 per cent of the available road space. This should be compared with

[3] *Source:* TRRL: *Research on Road Traffic* HMSO 1965 & L.R. 413 1971.
[4] *Bikeways: The State of the Art.* Washington DC: US Dept of Transportation, 1974.
[5] Eric Claxton, at the time Chief Engineer for Stevenage Development Corporation.

the bicycle, which takes up roughly the same proportion of road space as its proportion of journeys.[6]

Regular exercise has been shown to lessen tension, increase people's efficiency at work and improve sleep.[7] The advantage of cycling is that it has a purpose in addition to being a means of taking regular exercise. For recreational purposes, the bicycle provides freedom of movement coupled with direct contact with the environment.

The bicycle is virtually silent in operation[8] and it causes no pollution.[9]

1.3 The disadvantages of the bicycle

However, there are a number of disadvantages of cycling which require consideration. Between 8-9 am and 5-6 pm it rains on average, in any spot in the UK, on 12 days of the year.[10] To be caught cycling in heavy rain is an unpleasant experience that is only somewhat

[6] Taking into account the size of a vehicle, its stopping distance, parking space, and the delay caused to other traffic, the following picture emerges of the modal split for journeys to work in Central London:

Table 1.1

	% modal split	Land use (sq.m.min)	% of road space
Car driver	8·07	996·8	85·4
Car passenger	3·29	21·04	1·8
Motorcycle driver	0·93	62·38	5·3
Motorcycle passenger	0·04	–	–
Bus	10·39	76·42	6·5
Bicycle	0·35	3·1	0·3
Pedestrian	24·56	7·0	0·6
Tube	24·11	–	–
British Rail	28·27	–	–

Source: Central London Traffic Census: London Transport, 1976.

[7] *Fitness on 40 Minutes a Week.* M. Curruthers. 1976.

[8] The Transport and Road Research Laboratory predicts that if traffic growth continues, the proportion of the urban population suffering from unacceptable noise levels (in excess of an L_{10} level of 65 dB (A)) will increase from 46 per cent in 1970 to 61 per cent in 1980.

[9] This should be compared with the nuisance caused by other motor transport. The 1972-73 Road Traffic and Environment Survey showed that 14 per cent of 6,000 respondents noticed traffic fumes at home and 7 per cent were bothered by them; 71 per cent noticed 'dust and dirt' and 61 per cent were bothered by this; and 47 per cent were bothered by traffic fumes. The pollution caused by bicycle manufacture is negligible compared with that caused by the production of any other form of transport.

[10] *Richard's Bicycle Book.* Richard Ballantine. London: Pan, 1972.

ameliorated by the precautions of rainwear. Steep hills also present problems since bicycles can only be cycled up limited gradients. This difficulty is reflected in the fact that there are more bicycles per household in East Anglia (52 per cent) than in Wales (15 per cent). Strong winds can make cycling difficult and, in heavy traffic, dangerous. In fact, wind may be a greater deterrent to cyclists than steep hills or heavy rain. Other disadvantages, which could be partially overcome by improved design, include the susceptibility of bicycles to theft and their limited carrying capacity.

1.4 Conflict with the motor car

The bicycle has many advantages as a means of transport. It is the conflict between the bicycle and motorised transport, and between the bicycle and a road system designed for the motor car, that turns some of the advantages of cycling into disadvantages.

Travelling in urban areas by any means of transport is a nervous strain. However, the strain of travelling by car (heart rates can double)[11] is greater than cycling, and it is the presence of these cars that causes the strain on the cyclist. Although car fumes can be dangerous when inhaled in large quantities, it is likely that their greatest effect is as a deterrent to potential cyclists and a nuisance to current cyclists.

Broadly speaking, roads are designed to maximise their carrying capacity for high speed vehicles. This objective is incompatible with design for the needs of cyclists. For example, one way systems and free flow junctions increase the capacity of a road system but direct the cyclist on unnecessary detours and into dangerous manoeuvres.

Car drivers are often inconsiderate in their attitudes to cyclists. However, the fact that cyclists' rights are more respected in towns where cycling is prevalent suggests that an increase in the number of cyclists on all roads would condition car drivers to expect and allow for them.

1.5 Integrating cars and bicycles

Cycling can be made very much safer without recourse to complete segregation of bicycles from motorised transport. In many areas there

[11] *The Western Way of Death.* M. Curruthers. London: Davis-Poynter, 1974.

Figure 1.2 Cycling in London.

will be a large number of backstreets that could be made available only to cyclists and pedestrians (except for vehicular access). These backstreets, coupled with footpaths, combined bus and cycle lanes, and routes through parks and open land, will be the basic tools for adapting existing cities. These networks of cycle routes should link major traffic generators (places where journeys begin and end) but, where the bicycle does have to compete with other road traffic, careful attention can, and should, still be paid to the needs of cyclists.

In towns where greater restrictions are placed on cars, cyclists and pedestrians could be given priority in the transport system. Roads would be narrower and pavements broader and less cluttered with large and unsightly signposts. Some provision would be required to allow access for delivery and essential service vehicles, and some form of public transport would operate to give mobility to non-cyclists. Land released from car parks and garaging could be used for recreation, housing or simply as open space. Such a town becomes a place designed for people rather than cars. However, the widespread application of this type of approach will require substantial changes in the attitudes of national and local government.

1.6 Government policy

The greatest constraint on the construction of cycling facilities is the difficulty of generating the political will to create change. 'There is a great future for the bicycle if you make conditions right. If you make them wrong there isn't any future' (Ernest Marples, Minister of Transport 1968). The problem is that both national and local government lack the political courage to commit themselves to a thorough and positive policy of encouraging and financing allocation of facilities for cyclists wherever possible.

The Government Consultation Paper on Transport Policy gave evidence of no more than a passing interest in bicycles and quoted without qualification the statistic that bicycles are ten times as dangerous as cars, per mile travelled. The following statement was a very short part of the complete document, and we quote it in full:

10.9 Suggestions have been put forward from time to time that special roads should be constructed – or reserved within the existing road system – for pedal bicycles. Local authorities are responsible for the safe and convenient movement of people and goods in their areas and must consider what share of the available resources should go to making movement safer for the more vulnerable road users, including cyclists. There is scope for giving cyclists a safer ride on the existing roads, and the Government are encouraging several local authority experiments with this object. Only in new towns is it likely to be possible to construct a special system of cycleways; elsewhere it could hardly be justified unless large numbers of people, who would otherwise have used the general road system, could be attracted to use the cycleway system, but in areas where there are large numbers of people making journeys from home to work, or school, over a short distance (say under three miles) this condition might be fulfilled. The existing cycleway system at Stevenage is available for study, and a similar comprehensive system is planned in Peterborough. These offer starting points for further experiments and the Government will support schemes put forward by other authorities which promise benefits commensurate with their cost and which can be financed within available resources.

11.3 Pedal cycles provide cheap personal transport and, unlike motorcycles, do not cause pollution or create excessive noise. They save energy, except that of the cyclist. But for every mile driven they are 10 times as dangerous as cars, and are especially vulnerable in heavy traffic. They will continue to be widely used for sport and leisure, but real encouragement of their use for journeys to work in crowded city centres would need to be accompanied by extensive and sometimes costly segregation measures. Only on short local journeys can they be expected to be a serious alternative to public transport or to the car. They can, and do, provide a useful reserve in rural and semi-rural areas. Where the right conditions are found, local authorities will be justified in examining the economic case for diverting some of their available resources to improving facilities for cyclists.[12]

However, the government's Transport Policy White Paper[13] which followed the Consultation Document represented a small but significant change in policy. Rather than commenting on cycling

[12] *Transport Policy – A Consultation Document.* London, HMSO, 1976.
[13] *Transport Policy.* London, HMSO, 1977:
'128 The increasing cost of travel has led more people to think of cycling as a cheap and convenient way of getting about, and more would no doubt cycle if conditions were made safer and more pleasant. Completely segregated cycle routes would be impracticable or far too expensive in most cities, but local authorities should consider ways of helping cyclists when preparing traffic management schemes. Some local authorities have marked out lightly-used streets as cycle routes and more of this could be done when the roads are

facilities, the government requested local authorities to 'consider ways of helping cyclists' and to 'identify their proposals for such schemes in their annual transport policies and programmes'. As their part of the bargain, the government proposes to 'contribute to the cost of selective experimental schemes'. It is also worth noting that the White Paper recognises the importance of conserving oil supplies[14] and, more importantly, that we should aim to reduce our absolute dependence on motor transport.[15]

These policies will have to be vigorously applied if this country is to approach the level of bicycle provision in the rest of Europe.[16] Government policy has significantly influenced cycling provisions on the continent, and a similar approach in this country will require a considerably more positive attitude than has yet been demonstrated by the Department of Transport (DTp). Its contribution is limited to three documents, one giving outline guidelines,[17] one giving details of the signs that may (or may not) be used to sign bicycle facilities,[18] and the last giving ideas for the planning of new residential areas.[19]

We quote the Introduction and Summary to the outline guidelines in full, as evidence of the extreme caution shown by the Department:

> The publication of this note *does not imply* that the Department of the Environment is *advocating expenditure* on provision for cyclists. The need for provision is a matter for local authorities to consider within their overall transport budget.

[14] *Transport Policy*, Para 17.
[15] *Transport Policy*, Para 35.
[16] See Chapter 5.
[17] *Provisions for Cyclists*. London, DOE, 1975.
[18] *Signing for Cyclists*. London, DOE, 1976.
[19] *Residential Roads and Footpaths*. London, DTp, 1977.

---

suitable. More cycle stands in town centres and at or near public transport terminals would also help.

'129 Altogether, there is scope for many more practical initiatives, and for local authorities generally to take account of both pedestrian and cycle schemes which have been shown to be successful. Local authorities will be asked to identify their proposals for such schemes in their annual transport policies and programmes. The Department of Transport will strengthen its Traffic Advisory Unit, whose work covers provision for pedestrians and cyclists as well as traffic management. The Department, with its Regional Offices, will improve its advice to local authorities on useful measures and make generally available examples of successful schemes. The Department will shortly publish advice about planning to help pedestrians. It will also contribute to the cost of selected experimental schemes for cyclists, and help to devise and monitor them.'

SUMMARY

A. In existing urban areas which are relatively flat *it is possible* that selected existing side streets can be freed from all but minimum access traffic and designated together to form cycle routes.

B. It *may be possible*, by the existence of open space or redevelopment, to construct new cycleways.

C. Major road crossing should be controlled and further work is being undertaken on the safest ways to do this, at different cost levels.

D. The majority of the standards given in this document are, for the present, *suggestions only*.[20]

E. Cycle parking provisions should be an important consideration in any plan.

F. Costs and benefits cannot be accurately estimated: the improved safety of cyclists should be a prime objective. Any resultant improvement of traffic flows in the major roads should be regarded solely as a bonus.

The technical note on signs shows only three signs which may be used without prior approval by the Department, so bicycle schemes wishing to use any other signs are subject to delays. The third document contains a fairly encouraging statement in the recommended guidelines for access networks.

The need to make special provision for cyclists should always be considered especially where peak vehicle flows are expected to exceed about 100 vph, where major segregated footpath routes serving local community facilities are proposed in the layout of the scheme, or where the scheme can contribute to the creation of a cycle network over a wider area. Separate cycle routes and shared routes with demarcated lanes for pedestrians may both have a part to play.

In general, however, it can be concluded that there is little evidence of a strong commitment to making provisions for cyclists. Indeed, it looks more as if the government's policy is a belated response to pressure from those local authorities who are interested in doing something.

Each local authority has a different attitude to cycling, but in general they appear to hide behind the popular myth that cyclists are few and declining in number, and that cycling is extremely dangerous. They argue that encouraging cycling would increase road

[20] Our emphasis.

accidents. Consequently, little provision has been made for cycling except in a few isolated cases.[21]

1.7 The potential for cycling in Britain

The position of the government and local authorities reflects a general image of cyclists as second class citizens, out of date, and a danger and a nuisance to other road users. Whilst there is much that can be done by planners, by cyclists and by road safety officers to encourage more respect for the wishes and needs of cyclists, a general change of attitude will be required because planning for motorised transport effectively plans against the bicycle. Any prediction of a reduction in bicycle-use thus becomes self-fulfilling.

However, the fact that 80 per cent of all journeys are under five miles, that cycling is the fastest means of urban transport for journeys under four miles, and that all other forms of transport have become progressively more expensive, suggest that cycling could play an important role in future transport systems. It is our contention that if a small proportion of transport expenditure was used to provide facilities for cyclists, and if all possible opportunities for encouraging cycling are grasped, then the potential for an accelerating return to bicycles becomes a reality.

[21] See Chapter 6.

2/Bicycle usage

Until very recently cyclists were widely believed to be a tiny and still declining section of the community. Today, however, there can be no justification for that view. There is every indication not only that the decline in cyclists' numbers has halted, but also that cycling is on the increase once again. More importantly, it is being realised that cyclists were never such a tiny minority as was sometimes thought. To provide a clearer picture of the current level of bicycle usage this chapter examines official statistics on usage as well as other sources of information which show that official statistics are often rather misleading. It then goes on to discuss the potential for and constraints on growth in usage in the future.

2.1 Statistics on bicycle usage

When discussing official statistics on cycling it is necessary to realise from the outset that those statistics are usually produced as by-products of the collection of statistics on motor vehicles, particularly cars. The surveys mounted to do this are designed to give the best information possible on cars and other motor vehicles – any additional information provided on cycling is a useful bonus but of subsidiary importance. This is not to imply that cycling statistics are necessarily inaccurate or misleading but in practice a number of unfortunate defects appear in them because bicycles do not generally show the same characteristics as motor vehicles on the roads. They tend to use quieter roads, or even paths and cycle tracks.

Usage of different modes of transport in the UK is usually measured officially by the number of vehicle kilometres or miles travelled annually by each mode. These figures are published regularly in such publications as the *Annual Abstract of Statistics* and *Passenger Transport in Great Britain*, and show cycling declining steadily until 1975, in parallel with a similar decline in the usage of two-wheeled motor vehicles until 1972, and a steady increase in the usage of cars and taxis (see Fig. 2.1).

These are the statistics most frequently quoted, by government, local authorities and others, to describe trends in usage of different types of transport and the relative importance of each in the total system of passenger transport. Vehicle mileage is quite a good measure of the scale of the problem of catering for different types of

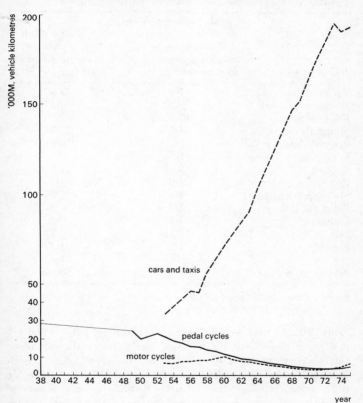

Figure 2.1 Vehicle kilometres annually by various forms of transport.

Source: Annual Abstract of Statistics (Pre-1963 estimates based on *Index Vehicle Mileage: Road Accidents*, 1966, Table 1).

vehicles and of their impact on the community; the greater the
mileage done by a particular vehicle type the more roadspace needs to
be devoted to it and the greater the impact of noise, pollution, etc. A
rather better measure, and one that is quite often quoted, is the
number of passenger (as opposed to vehicle) miles travelled by each
type of transport. Approximate figures on passenger mileage can be

Table 2.1   Bicycle usage for different journey purposes

Journey purpose	Number of journeys made all or part by bicycle as a percentage of all passenger journeys in road vehicles[1]	Percentage of all bicycle journeys made for different purposes
To and from work	7·4	37·6
In course of work	2·0	1·8
Education	10·6	12·2
Shopping	4·5	13·7
Personal business	6·3	10·8
Eating and drinking	1·3	0·8
Social	3·3	11·1
Entertainment	2·9	2·1
Sport (participating)	7·2	2·8
Sport (watching)	2·4	0·3
Holidays	0·7	0·2
Day trips	13·1	5·1
Escorting	1·2	1·3
All purposes	5·2	100%

Source: National Travel Survey, 1975-76.
[1] Includes surface passenger travel only.

easily deduced from vehicle mileage by assuming 1·0, 1·4 and 1·1
passengers per vehicle for bicycles, cars and two-wheeled motor
vehicles respectively. However, there are two major defects in both
passenger and vehicle mileage figures. Firstly, these figures do not
really reflect the value to individuals of particular types of transport.
People travel to gain access to something, be it a school, shop, factory
or friend's home. For this purpose a short journey fulfils a need just as
well as a longer one. In other words, the number of journeys made
annually by each type of transport gives a much better indication of
the value of each to individuals. Table 2.1 shows the number of

journeys by bicycle as a percentage of all journeys made by different types of passenger transport, for a variety of different journey purposes.

The table shows that cycling is of rather greater importance as a means of personal transport than the usual official statistics suggest.

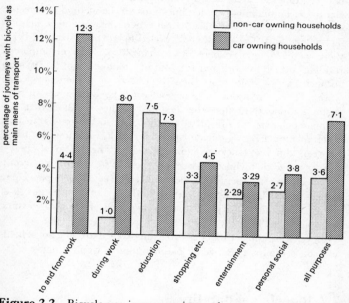

Figure 2.2 Bicycle use in car-owning and non-car-owning households.

Source: National Travel Survey 1975-76
Note: Excludes walks of less than one mile

Some 5·2 per cent of all journeys by road passenger vehicle are made all or part by bicycle, compared with only 1·9 per cent of road passenger vehicle mileage made by bicycle in 1976. Surprisingly too, the *National Travel Survey* suggested that more journeys are made all or part by bicycle than by British Rail and London Transport Underground combined.

The second defect in vehicle mileage statistics is that they are very likely to be underestimates. They are based on monthly traffic counts carried out by the Department of Transport which do not include estate roads, bridle paths or cycle tracks, so that any growth in cycling on these will not be reflected at all in official statistics.

So far all the statistics discussed refer only to the national situation. However, these statistics mask wide variations in bicycle usage between different areas and different types of household. The 1971 Census of Population included questions on the method of travel to work[1] and revealed that whilst 4·4 per cent of the working population of England and Wales as a whole cycled to work regularly in 1971, there were 26 towns where more than 20 per cent of employed residents cycled to work and 178 (out of a total of about 1,350) local authority areas where more than 10 per cent of residents cycled to work. These variations may be explained by differences in local custom, topography and other factors but they do show that in a number of areas cycling plays a major role in the total transport system. Similarly, aggregate statistics mask variations in usage between different socio-economic groups. The National Travel Survey found that whilst 3 per cent of those in socio-economic group A cycled to work, 5 per cent, 7 per cent, 11 per cent and 14 per cent in groups B, C, D and E respectively did so. Differences in use of bicycles are equally marked between car-owning and non-car-owning households, as Fig. 2.2 shows.

Bicycles are thus of much greater importance to some households and social groups than overall national figures would suggest.

2.2 Bicycle availability

So much for current usage of bicycles. What potential is there for future growth? One indication of this could be the extent of bicycle ownership, on the grounds that owning a bicycle is a necessary precondition for using one. Unfortunately, accurate figures on the number of bicycles owned or in use are unobtainable since there is no compulsory registration for bicycles as there is for cars. Estimates of bicycle ownership vary widely, as Table 2.2 shows, one explanation being the way in which unused and unserviceable bicycles and children's bicycles are treated in the survey.

However, all sources indicate that there are more than 7 million bicycles in the UK, and it is likely that there are substantially more.

[1] See Census 1971, *Workplace and Transport to Work Tables*. London: HMSO.

This compares with a total car ownership in 1976 of 14 million.

Information on bicycle sales suggests that the number of bicycles in Britain is increasing rapidly. The Bicycle Association of Great Britain produces annual estimates of the numbers of bicycles sold in the UK, including imported models. These show sales in recent years increasing annually by about 12 per cent from 550,000 in 1970 to over 1·1 million in 1976. The proportion of adult models in those figures also increased from 35 per cent in 1970 to 50 per cent in 1976. The 1·1 million bicycles sold in the UK in 1976 compare with 1·25 million new car registrations. It therefore seems that the growth in numbers of bicycles is parallel with that of the car.

Table 2.2 Estimates of bicycle ownership in the UK

Source	Year of estimate	Bicycles owned
British Cycling Bureau	1973	15 million
British Cycling Bureau	1973	12 million on the road
Bicycle Association	1973	11 million in use
Mintel Market Intelligence	1973	7 million
National Travel Survey	1975-76	7·2 million
National Opinion Polls Ltd	1976	13·7 million

An alternative measure of availability of bicycles, and the potential for increased usage, is the number of households in the UK owning bicycles. The National Travel Survey showed 24 per cent of households in the UK owning bicycles in 1975, varying from only 15 per cent in Wales to 52 per cent in East Anglia (see Fig. 2.3). A National Opinion Poll survey in 1976 showed 42 per cent of households in the UK owning bicycles, the difference probably being accounted for by the inclusion of children's bicycles in this survey. By comparison, 55 per cent of UK households owned cars in 1975.

2.3 The potential for growth in bicycle usage

In the longer term the potential for growth in bicycle usage will depend less upon current availability of bicycles than upon changing attitudes to the bicycle and the national economic situation. Thus, whilst some would advocate that the recent upsurge in bicycle usage is the start of a continuing trend and others believe that it is no more

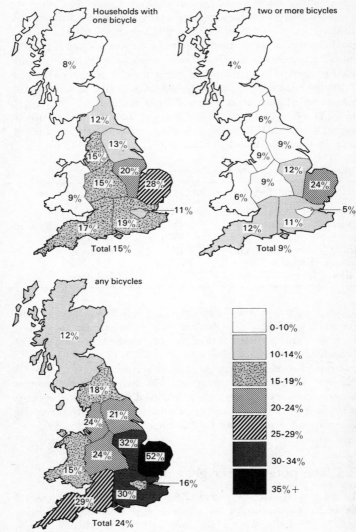

Figure 2.3   Bicycle ownership by geographical area.

than a minor 'hiccup' in the continuing decline in cycling, any such statements are necessarily merely speculative. However, examination of the physical constraints on using a bicycle and recent evidence of attitudes to cycling show that there is no reason why bicycle usage should not continue to grow, given either the will to encourage it or an economic situation conducive to this growth.

Physical constraints are often cited as reasons why the use of bicycles could not become more widespread; it is argued that cycling is restricted to the relatively young and fit, that the weather is not always amenable or that many places are too hilly for cycling, and that

Table 2.3   Distance of journeys to work using different modes

% of journeys of less than:	Mode of travel						
	Train	Bus	Car	Bicycle	Walk[1]	Motorcycle	All
1 mile	0	2	4	21	—	4	4
2 miles	1	20	19	63	85	23	26
3 miles	3	34	33	80	97	44	40
5 miles	10	69	55	94	100	68	60
10 miles	41	94	81	100	100	89	82
15 miles	62	99	91	100	100	96	90
25 miles	79	100	97	100	100	99	95

Source: *National Travel Survey*, 1975-76.
[1] Excludes walks of less than one mile.

most journeys are too long to be made by bicycle. Certainly such constraints do have a major influence, as is shown by the low level of bicycle ownership in relatively hilly Wales, compared with the high level in East Anglia. But it would be wrong to attach too great importance to physical factors. They are not significantly different now from what they were in the 1930s when cycling was far more widespread, so they can hardly be expected to act as major constraints on increased bicycle usage. The only factors which may have changed are the age, distribution and fitness of the population and the average length of journeys.

It is certainly true that there is now a greater proportion of elderly people in the population than ever before, but the increase in their numbers is not such as to make the bicycle unsuited to a large proportion of the population. In any case cycling is not confined to the young. A survey in Camden in 1974[2] found that 14 per cent of 322 cyclists surveyed were over 50 years old and 6 per cent over 60. This was in an area of London where cycling conditions were relatively bad, so that cycling would be expected to be more than usually confined to the young and adventurous.

With progressive improvements in the ease and relative cost of travel, average journey distances have increased over the years. To what extent these increases mean that the bicycle is no longer appropriate for many journeys is difficult to gauge. But data from the National Travel Survey of 1975-76 on journeys to work, the most common type of journey made by bicycle, show (Table 2.3) that there are still many journeys of short enough length to be made by bicycle.

On the basis of the data produced in the Survey, if only 10 per cent of journeys to work by car of less than 5 miles were made instead by bicycle, the total number of journeys to work by bicycle would increase by some 50 per cent. Such a moderate switch away from cars is by no means inconceivable.

2.4 Attitudes to cycling

Changes in people's attitudes to using bicycles are likely to be much more important in determining future growth in bicycle usage. The decline in bicycle usage over the past 25 years was caused both by people's attitudes and by public policy.

Whilst hard attitudinal evidence is not available, it is likely that attitudes to cycling are beginning to change, evidenced amongst other things by the recent rapid growth in bicycle sales.

Table 2.4 shows the replies of 2,006 respondents when asked, without prompting, what action would do most to make people want to use their bicycles more often.

This survey suggests that on the one hand the greatest impetus to more people taking up cycling is higher costs of alternative means of travel, and on the other hand that the greatest deterrent to this is the danger and unpleasantness of sharing roads with fast moving traffic.

It is likely that both fares and petrol costs will continue to rise in the foreseeable future. This seems to be accepted in the government's

[2] 'Planning for the Bicycle' (1974). E. Ann Shamash. Unpublished Diploma Thesis (Polytechnic of Central London).

Table 2.4   Attitudes to increased cycle usage

Action which would make more people use bicycles	% of respondents citing action
Less traffic/safer conditions	19 ⎤
Bicycle lanes on streets	14 ⎦ 33
Higher petrol costs	13 ⎤
Increased public transport fares	12 ⎦ 25
Keep fit	6
Increased car costs	5
Cuts in public transport service	4
Fine weather, no other means of travel, cycling for pleasure	2 of each
Parking for bicycles, cheaper bicycles, shortage or lack of petrol, for convenience, roads made less hilly	1 of each
Don't know	17

Source: National Opinion Polls Limited, 1976.

recent White Paper on Transport Policy. The rises will create further potential demand for cycling. Whether or not this potential is fully realised will depend on the extent to which local authorities recognise that bicycles are an essential means of transport to certain groups of people and create conditions that are both safe and attractive.

3/Bicycle safety

Cycling is generally regarded as a rather dangerous activity – 'ten times as dangerous as driving a car for every mile travelled' according to the government's recent Consultation Document on Transport Policy. However, as was seen in the last chapter, the real situation is not always all that the official statistics blandly indicate. This chapter reviews accident statistics, pointing out their defects, and shows that they are frequently misused to compare the safety records of cycling with other forms of transport, and to justify present public policy towards cycling. It concludes that whilst cycling *is* more dangerous than some methods of travel, though not to the extent that official statistics suggest, this need not necessarily continue to be the case.

3.1 Recent trends in cycling safety

The numbers of cyclists killed or seriously injured on the roads has declined fairly steadily over the last few years. In 1964 583 were killed and 8,048 seriously injured, compared with 300 killed and 4,631 seriously injured in 1976 (Fig. 3.1).

However, the amount of cycling being done has also declined steadily over the years (see Fig. 2.1) so that cycling has not necessarily been getting safer for those who have continued to keep it up. Some other measure than total casualties, which incorporates the effect of changes in the amount of cycling, is therefore necessary to show safety trends over the years. Such a measure is provided by the rate of cyclist casualties per passenger mile. These are the most commonly used indicator of trends in safety, and are shown in Fig. 3.2.

3.2 Defects in accident statistics

These statistics suffer from a number of defects which mean that they are at best only crude indicators of trends and should be interpreted with great care. The first defect is that many bicycle accidents are never reported to the police, upon whose records official statistics are based. The driver of a motor vehicle involved in an accident in which someone is injured must, by law, inform the police, but cyclists are not required to do this. It is impossible to estimate the extent of

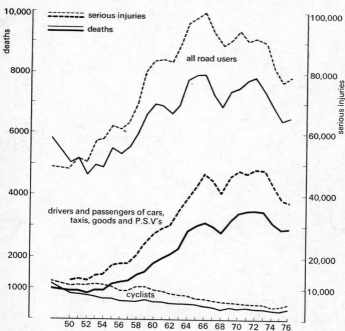

Figure 3.1   Trends in road user casualties

Source: *Road Accidents in Great Britain 1974*. London: HMSO

unrecorded bicycle accidents, but it would probably be safe to say that the more serious the accident the less likely it is to go unreported. Most reliance can therefore be placed on statistics for fatal and serious injuries to cyclists, particularly where motor vehicles are involved, so this chapter concentrates on these.

A second defect in the official statistics is that they provide scant basis for apportioning blame. Except for the drunken cyclist who skids, loses control, or wraps himself around a lamp-post, bicycle accidents occur because of the mixing of cycles with motor traffic. It would be as true to say that a particular accident between a car and a bicycle would not have occurred if the car had not been there as it would to say that it would not have occurred if the cyclist had not been around. But official statistics, which show that a certain number of cyclists are killed for every million miles cycled, tend to lead to the

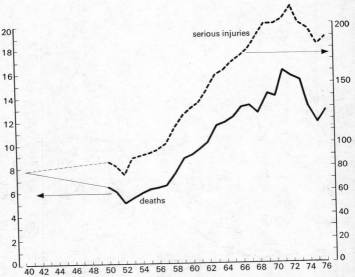

Figure 3.2 Deaths and serious injuries per 100 million passenger miles travelled

Source: Road Accidents in Great Britain 1974. London: HMSO.

latter interpretation – that those cyclists would not have been killed had those million miles not been cycled. This statement is obviously true, but it only presents half the picture. A Metropolitan Police study[1] of 239 accidents to adult cyclists in 1974, which estimated that the cyclist was mainly to blame in 31 per cent of the accidents, but that the other road users (mainly car, van and lorry drivers) were

[1] *Pedal Cyclist Casualties in London*, Metropolitan Police (B5 Branch) B5/14/75 (see Appendix III).

responsible for nearly twice as many (58 per cent) of the accidents, puts the matter further into perspective.

A third defect is that the number of vehicle or passenger miles travelled is not necessarily the best measure of exposure to risk of accident for cycling. It could be argued that cyclists are at risk all the time that they are on the road. In this case total passenger *time* spent cycling would be a better measure of exposure to risk. Alternatively, since most cycle accidents occur at or near road junctions, the total numbers of cyclists passing through a road junction might be used as a measure of the danger of that junction. In this calculation the safety of a cyclist depends on the number of junctions he travels through. Strictly speaking, no measure is any more or less valid than any other. Total passenger mileage is used in official statistics because the statistics are readily available, not because it is in any way the best measure. So long as it is only used to compare safety trends in cycling year by year this is not likely to lead to problems, since total passenger mileage cycled, total time spent cycling or total number of cyclists crossing junctions are all likely to vary in proportion to one another. But problems do arise when it is used to compare the safety of cycling with that of other modes of transport.

3.3 Comparisons between bicycle and car safety levels

The defects in official statistics listed so far only mean that they are of limited reliability, not that the statistics in themselves are wrong. Misleading conclusions *are* frequently drawn, however, when official statistics are used as a basis for comparing the safety of different forms of transport, particularly cars and bicycles.

The argument is that when a person is faced with the choice of making a particular journey by car or bicycle, say, the casualty rate per passenger mile travelled by each is the best available measure of the comparative risks of making that journey. The actual risk of accident on the journey will be the casualty rate of the method of travel he chooses multiplied by the length of the journey. Thus, a cyclist making a particular journey in 1974 would expect to be ten times as likely to be killed as someone driving a car or taxi to make that journey. So far as it goes this line of reasoning is valid – but there are four important limitations.

Firstly, as already noted, passenger miles travelled are not necessarily the best measure of exposure to risk of accident for cycling, nor for any other form of transport. They merely provide a *convenient* basis for comparison, since the statistics are available for most forms of transport.

Secondly, the choice between cycling and driving a car is not always the simple one of whether to make a particular journey by one or the other. If deciding between buying a car or bicycle as a means of

Table 3.1   Comparison of cyclist casualties with mileage cycled by age group

Age group	No. of casualties	Rate per 100,000 population in group	% of all casualties	Estimate of mileage cycled by age group[1]
0-4	164	4	0·8	0·4
5-9	2,516	58	12	4·3
10-14	6,727	150	32·0	21·0
15-19	3,324	83	15·8	13·0
20-29	2,015	26	9·6	11·5
30-59	4,186	22	19·9	37·5
60-69	1,414	24	6·7	11·6
70+	634	13	3·0	—
Unknown	5	—	—	—
All ages	20,985	39	100%	100%

Sources: *Road Accidents in Great Britain 1975. National Travel Survey 1975/76.*
[1] This is a rough estimate because the mileage figures are produced for a different set of age groups.

getting about, one would be more interested in the risk of injury during the course of a year using one or the other method of travel. But a cyclist might reasonably expect to travel some 2,000 miles annually, whereas a motorist might do some 10,000 miles.[2] Thus if the cyclist were ten times as likely to have an accident per mile travelled he would be only *twice* as likely to have an accident as the motorist during the course of a year's travel.

A third, and more serious, limitation is that official statistics on casualty rates of cyclists and car drivers do not include the same things

[2] The cyclist may make longer journeys by public transport, but these are relatively safe and do not significantly affect the data.

in them. The rates for cyclists include casualties to all age groups, whilst those for cars overwhelmingly consist of casualties to over 17-year-olds. Yet, as Table 3.1 and Fig. 3.3 show, many cyclist casualties occur in the younger age groups – 10 to 14-year-olds experience seven times as many cyclist casualties as the over 20s.

Better evidence of the accident risks for different age groups comes from a comparison of casualties in each age group with the proportion of miles cycled by that age group. Table 3.1 shows that all age groups under 20 were involved in a greater proportion of accidents than the proportion of miles they cycled, whereas all groups over 20 were involved in a smaller proportion of accidents than mileage cycled. Thus the official statistics seriously exaggerate the risk of cycling for people over 20 years old.

A final limitation on the use of official statistics to compare cycling safety with that of cars or other methods of travel, is that the statistics refer only to casualties on all classes of road. But someone deciding whether to make a particular journey by car or cycle would ideally wish to know the risk of accident on the particular types of road he will be using. Table 3.2 shows that cycling on minor roads is generally speaking much safer than on major roads.

Table 3.2   Cyclist casualty rates on different classes of road

Class of Road	Fatal casualties per 100 million cycle kilometres		All casualties per 100 million cycle kilometres		Ratio of cyclist to car driver fatal casualty rate	
	Urban	Rural	Urban	Rural	Urban	Rural
'A'	15·3	30·2	1,006	580	21·8	20·1
'B'	6·8	9.8	716	369	9·7	12·2
'C' and unclassified	3·3	3·8	436	222	11·0	7·6
All classes	6·8	10·4	613	320	13·6	8·7

Source: Transport and Road Research Laboratory Report LR394.

Car travel on minor roads is safer too, although a cyclist is 7·6 times as likely to be killed as a car driver on a rural 'C' road, but 21·8 times more likely on an urban 'A' road.

In conclusion, using official accident statistics to compare the dangers of cycling with using other forms of transport can be very misleading, making statements such as that in the government's

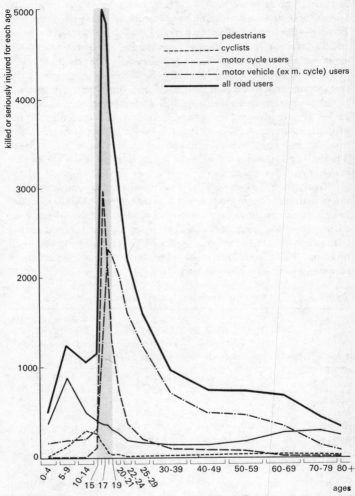

Figure 3.3 Deaths and serious injuries for different means of transport by age group

Source: *Transport Statistics of Great Britain*. London: HMSO.

Green Paper on Transport Policy quoted earlier effectively meaningless. This is not to say that cycling is safe – it may be safer relative to driving a car than the statistics suggest, but driving a car is not a particularly safe occupation itself compared with sitting in a bus or train. The point is that official statistics do not give a particularly useful basis for assessing the dangers of cycling. In particular, if you are over 20 and cycle mainly on minor urban roads, breathe again – cycling is not nearly as dangerous as a first reading of the statistics would suggest.

3.4 Statistics as a basis for public policy

So far cycling safety has only been discussed from the point of view of the cyclist or the intending cyclist assessing the personal danger of undertaking a journey. But on what basis should public policy on cycling be determined? At the moment, it seems, this is decided on the same basis as for the individual traveller. Cycling is seen to be much more dangerous than other methods of travel (for the traveller), so it is concluded by many local authorities that anything they might do to encourage cycling would also effectively encourage more accidents. They argue that it is better to let cyclists' numbers continue declining, so that accidents will decline as well.

When determining public policy towards cycling, however, it should be the risks to the whole community which are taken into account, not just the risks to those actually travelling by bicycle, car or whatever. We have shown that cyclists themselves are the main casualties in accidents involving themselves and other road users. But in accidents involving cars, other road users, particularly pedestrians and cyclists, are likely to be the casualties. In other words, a cyclist may run a relatively high risk of being injured himself on a particular journey, but is unlikely to cause anyone else to be injured, whereas the opposite is true for the motorist. Figures on the safety of cycling compared with travelling by car look very different when the risks to the whole community are taken into account. Fig. 3.4 shows the mean distances which different types of vehicle travel before being involved in an accident in which the vehicle occupant or anyone else is injured.

On this basis 100 miles cycled are likely to lead to only 2·8 times as many fatal accidents (most of them involving cyclists as the main casualty) as 100 miles travelled by a car. Bearing in mind, too, that these figures do not distinguish between differing classes of roads or different age groups involved in accidents, it will be seen that cycling is not always the thoroughly dangerous activity some authorities seem to believe.

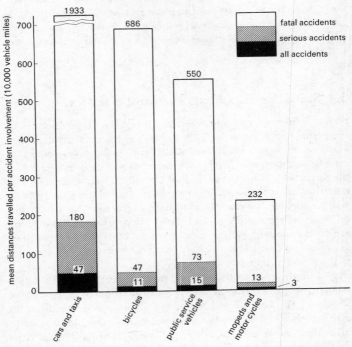

Figure 3.4   Mean distances travelled per accident involvement

Source: *Road Accidents in Great Britain 1974*.
Note: One or more casualties may occur in one accident so these figures are not directly comparable with those in Figure 3.2; on average 1·08 fatal casualties and 1·23 serious casualties occur in each fatal and serious accident.

The 'Road Safety' argument – that authorities should not encourage cycling, for fear of increasing the numbers of accidents – is further discredited when the cost of saving lives by transferring travel from bicycles to other forms of transport such as the car is considered. Reducing bicycle mileage by 27·5 million miles will save four lives, but if this mileage is done by car instead then one more life will be lost. In fact it is necessary for 10 million passenger miles to be transferred from bicycle to car for there to be a net saving of one life.

Broadly speaking, roads are justified on the grounds that an estimate of the total saving to people has to be greater than the construction cost of the road. Saving one life by transferring 10 million cycled miles to cars costs £350,000[3] (assuming car running costs to be 5p per mile). Thus, the construction of facilities to make cycling safer would be a much cheaper way of saving lives.

3.5 Conclusion for public policy on cycling

This chapter has only been able to point to some of the more glaring weaknesses and deficiencies in official cycling safety statistics. It has shown that, as currently used, these statistics provide a totally inadequate basis for determining public policy towards cycling, but it is beyond our scope to suggest an alternative basis. What is needed is a complete reappraisal of the safety of cycling compared with other forms of travel, taking into account:

(i) The different age groups involved in accidents and the importance of different modes of transport to each age group;

(ii) the usage of different classes of road;

(iii) the risks to the whole community which result from the use of a particular mode of transport;

(iv) the cost of saving lives by discouraging cycling and encouraging other forms of transport such as the car.

Such a reappraisal, needing a good deal of new research, would form a more suitable basis for determining public policy towards cycling.

It has not been argued in this chapter that cycling is in fact safe. So long as some 200-300 cyclists are tragically killed on the roads each year this obviously cannot be so. Safety comparisons have mainly

[3] Statistical explanation: Looking at Fig. 3.4 it will be seen that reducing bicycle mileage by $6·86 \times 10^6$ vehicle miles will save one fatal accident. But if cars are used instead of bicycles to do this amount of travel this will result in a further 0·25 fatal accidents occurring, or 0·27 fatal casualties. It is in fact necessary for $9·85 \times 10^6$ passenger miles of travel to be transferred from bicycle to car for there to be a net saving of one life. Since average car occupancy is 1·4, this travel results in $7·03 \times 10^6$ vehicle miles of car traffic, which – assuming the running costs of cars to be 5p per mile – represents a cost of some £350,000.

been drawn between the car and the bicycle because this is the comparison most often made in official statements. But if cycling is still dangerous, even allowing for the inadequacy of the statistics, there is no reason why this should continue in the future.

3.6 Future prospects for cycling safety

There are a number of reasons why the current level of cycling safety may improve in the future. The first two reasons are likely to operate independently of whatever policies are adopted towards cycling.

First of all, there is good evidence to suggest that the current resurgence in cycling consists predominantly of adults taking to the bicycle again in view of its economic, health and sporting advantages. The proportion of adult models in cycle sales has been rising and current promotional efforts are aimed primarily at the adult population. But it has already been suggested that the accident rate for adult cyclists is much lower than that for child cyclists, so that if the proportion of adults in the total cycling population increases in the future, as seems likely, overall accident rates are likely to decrease in consequence.

A second factor is that it might be expected that cycling is likely to increase more on quieter, minor roads than busy main roads. Again it has already been shown that cycling on minor roads is safer than on major roads, so that if the proportion of cycling done on them increases in future, the accident rate will again improve.

Most important, however, is the influence of local authority planning on safety. Cycling is relatively dangerous at present due to the need for cyclists to mix constantly with motor traffic. As the following chapters will show, there is enormous scope for increasing the degree of segregation between cyclists and motor traffic and hence improving safety.

There is also a great deal of scope for more education on safety. Current road safety campaigns concerned with cycling are aimed primarily at school children – and rightly so, in view of their high accident rates – and at cyclists to persuade them to make themselves more conspicuous to motor traffic, particularly at night. Whilst there is some value in this latter approach, since it is rather easier to focus a campaign on cyclists who are fewer in number than motorists and are more directly concerned with cycling safety, it is a somewhat misconceived one. The Metropolitan Police Study already cited suggested that 78 per cent of adult bicycle casualties occurred during daylight, that other road users were to blame in nearly twice as many accidents as cyclists, and that 79 per cent of accidents occurred at or near road junctions. This suggests that most accidents occurred because motorists either did not see a cyclist, did not expect to see one, or did not look in the right place for one when making turning movements at junctions. There is thus a strong case for directing safety campaigns to make motorists aware of the special problems of cyclists and to teach them to keep special watch for cyclists, particularly at junctions. Campaigns aimed at persuading cyclists to make themselves more conspicuous at night only relate to a small part of the problem.

Clearly a great deal more information than this is needed on which to base effective road safety campaigns and design safer facilities for cyclists. Appendix III reproduces part of the Metropolitan Police Study which gives further insights into a small sample of cycling accidents.

3.7 Conclusion

In conclusion there is no longer any excuse for official policy to continue to ignore cycling as a serious mode of transport on the grounds that it is too dangerous. This chapter has shown that cycling in many circumstances is not nearly as dangerous as official statistics suggest, and, more importantly, that it need not be so dangerous in future. In fact, it is the policies of many local authorities which ignore cycling and fail to provide facilities for it that are contributing to the dangers of cycling. Such policies can only dampen the significant resurgence of interest in cycling, and discourage potential users from taking to the bicycle.

4/Bicycle law

Having discussed the reasons for encouraging cycling, we now move on to the second part of our report and look at ways to make cycling a more attractive means of transport. However, before describing the facilities which could be provided to do this, it is important to recognise that some of the constraints on bicycle planning originate in the present law.

Bicycle law, like bicycle planning, has developed by accident rather than by design. This is because the highway law has evolved primarily to control motor vehicles, and bicycles have only been considered as an afterthought. Laws concerning bicycles have therefore been precariously linked with motor vehicle legislation. The result of this piecemeal approach is that the law concerning bicycles is spread amongst at least eleven major pieces of legislation and many more sets of regulations. It will therefore be particularly difficult to make substantial changes to bicycle law as so many Acts would need to be amended. More importantly, this complicated situation makes the level of public understanding of the law very low. It also discourages local authorities from making provisions for cyclists and has provided them with excuses for not designing facilities.

The aim of this chapter is to clarify some misunderstandings about bicycle law and to explain the present legal basis for the provision of cycle routes. Since the current law presents many problems, we conclude by looking at the possibility of making changes which would positively encourage bicycle planning.

4.1 Definitions

A prerequisite of any description and discussion of bicycle law is a clear understanding of the legal definitions of the terms used, since these statements form the basis for the interpretation of the law.

Starting with the most general term, *a vehicle* has been described as 'something in the nature of a carriage which is, or may be used, for the carriage of persons or things'.[1] This term will almost always include a cycle, though it does depend on the Act to which reference is being made. The term 'vehicle' is not defined in the statutes.

A *motor vehicle* is 'a mechanically propelled vehicle intended or adapted for use on roads'.[2] The term 'bicycle' is rarely mentioned in the relevant statutes and regulations. The most common term is *cycle* and this has been described in an old case as: 'a mechanical contrivance to facilitate the progress of foot passengers the motive power being supplied by the legs of the driver'.[3] A *bicycle* is defined similarly but must only have two wheels.[4]

Driving is another important term, which has been described in the following way: 'You drive if the vehicle, when moving, is subject to your control and direction'.[5] Therefore, walking a bicycle across the road may technically be driving it and, as will be shown later, this has some important repercussions.

A *highway* does not have a statutory definition. It has been described as 'a way over which all members of the public are entitled to pass and repass'.[6] The highway is a collective term which generally includes the carriageway (i.e. the road), the footway (i.e. the pavement), and in some places a cycle track[7] (see Fig. 4.1). However, it should be noted that footpaths, cycle routes and bridleways fall within the definition, so a highway need not include a carriageway.

A *carriageway* is defined as 'a way . . . over which the public have a right of way for the passage of vehicles (not including a cycle track)'.[8]

It is important to distinguish between a footpath and a footway. *A footway* is a way alongside a carriageway over which the public have a

[1] Equipment Investments *v.* Dowthwaite [1969] and Ellis *v.* Nott-Bower 13 TLR [1896].

[2] Road Traffic Act 1972 s. 190 (1).

[3] Smith *v.* Kynnersley [1903] 1 K.B. 755.

[4] These definitions do not include mopeds. See Motor Vehicles (Driving Licences) (Amendment) Regulations 1976, Para 3 (1) (c).

[5] *Stones Justices Manual* 1977, p. 3582. Note, this definition is not exhaustive. See, for example, R. *v.* Spindley (1961) Crim. L.R. 486, where it was held that when a vehicle is being pushed the person at the wheel is driving if he has a common design with the people pushing the vehicle, and R. *v.* MacDonagh (1974) QB448 (2AE257), where it was held that a person walking beside a vehicle which is being pushed or moving by gravity will not be driving merely because he has his hand on the steering wheel.

[6] Halsbury's Laws of England, 3rd edition, vol. 19, p. 12.

[7] See Chapter 7.2 for definition.

[8] Highways Act 1959 s. 295.

right of way on foot only.[9] *A footpath* is defined similarly but does not have to run alongside a road.[10]

The legal constraint on cyclists using anything other than carriageways is the Local Government Act 1888, which states:

> bicycles, tricycles, velocipedes and other similar machines are hereby declared to be carriages within the meaning of the Highway Acts.

Since the bicycle is treated as a 'carriage' in law it has to adhere to the laws for all other types of vehicles. The laws for vehicles place strict controls on their use in an attempt to make efficient use of road space,

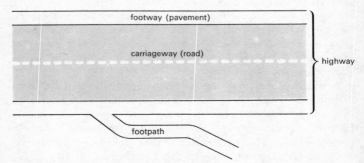

Figure 4.1 Highway terminology.

minimise the dangers of using roads, provide safety for pedestrians and create environmentally acceptable areas for shopping, recreation and other activities.

This approach has resulted in a truly massive loss of freedom for the cyclist. Rather than being allowed to cycle on all routes which are available for pedestrians, and only restricted from these routes where they present real dangers, the cyclist has been banned from these routes except in cases where particular paths have been opened up. However, as will be seen in Chapter 7.8, it is often perfectly acceptable to mix cyclists and pedestrians and to provide cycle routes on footpaths and pavements, on paths in parks, and in pedestrianised streets. We describe below the legal procedures which are available to make provisions in each of these situations, to demonstrate that it is a

[9] Highways Act 1959 s. 295.
[10] Road Traffic Act 1960 s. 257 (1) and Road Traffic Regulation Act 1967 s. 104.

cumbersome process to use these procedures for each and every cycle route.

4.2 Current problems

(i) *Footpaths and footways*

In urban areas many footpaths are dedicated by the highway authority, which in doing so takes on certain responsibilities for the care and maintenance of the footpath. A list of these paths should be available for inspection on a local register.

Under the Highway Act 1835, it is an offence to ride or drive a bicycle along footways but it is *not* a statutory offence to ride along public footpaths which do not run alongside a road. However, local authorities have the power to make bye-laws[11] or local traffic orders[12] to make it an offence in particular places. 'No cycling' signs will generally be displayed in these situations.

In many cases local authorities have made extreme use of these bye-laws, fearing large numbers of accidents between cyclists and pedestrians. It has not been recognised that the alternative, which is often a busy main road, is many times more dangerous. However, even where a local authority has been convinced that cyclists should be segregated from other motor traffic, there are legal difficulties in creating cycle routes.

The law is quite clear where a local authority wishes to create a cycle track along the side of a road. The Highways Act 1959 s. 66 gives them express powers to do this and the Road Traffic Regulation Act 1967 allows them to make orders to 'facilitate the passage of any class of traffic' and to prevent certain vehicles from using the highway. But there are many situations where neither space nor money exists to create such tracks. Alternative routes, which may not even go beside roads, will often be preferable. Unfortunately s. 66 does not cover this.

Under present law the legal mechanism for a local authority to create this type of route seems to be as follows. The Highways Act 1959 categorises a cycle track as a highway (s. 295(1)). Under s. 26 of

[11] All draft bye-laws require confirmation by the relevant Secretary of State, normally the DOE, before they can become valid.

[12] This power is given to local authorities under a variety of statutes; for example, under the Local Government Act 1972 s. 235 and under the Road Traffic Regulation Act 1967 s. 13.

this Act local authorities are given powers to create new highways. It therefore seems that they can make cycle routes by creating a highway and preventing all motor vehicles from using it. In this way it would be possible to create either an exclusive cycle path or a joint cycle-pedestrian path.

In certain circumstances it will be easier than this. For example, under the legislation governing new towns clearer powers exist for the creation of cycle or joint cycle-pedestrian paths, and this may explain why many more such routes have been created in new towns.

(ii) *Paths in parks*

Cycling is often not allowed in parks and other open spaces because children playing on bicycles could be a nuisance to the general public. Again, this forces cyclists to take detours along potentially more dangerous roads. One way round this is, for instance, to use s. 15 Open Spaces Act[13] which allows local authorities to make bye-laws to control the use of open spaces. In particular, they 'may admit persons and regulate the admission of such persons there as they think proper'. Local authorities could therefore pass bye-laws, restricting certain paths for the use of cyclists only, or forbidding playing on bicycles. However, when confirming bye-laws, the DOE strives for clarity and certainty (essential for a bye-law to be effective) and for uniformity, which may have the effect of stifling unusual proposals by a forward-thinking local authority.

(iii) *Pedestrianised streets*

Although pedestrianised streets are often closed to all types of vehicle, such streets can be made available to cyclists by prohibiting motor vehicles from entrance to the pedestrian area. The design of shared bicycle and pedestrian streets is discussed in Chapter 7. For legal purposes the road remains a highway from which certain classes of vehicle are excluded under the Road Traffic Regulation Act.

There are two other important current problems, the first relating to the legal basis for providing bicycle parking facilities, and the second to the problems of setting up barriers to through traffic at road closures. These are discussed in sections 7.7 and 7.5 respectively.

---

[13] Parks and open spaces, in practice, are governed by a mass of different legislation, depending on their locality and status. Powers to make similar bye-laws should exist in all situations.

4.3 Changing bicycle law

Clearly, the present law does not encourage planners to provide cycle routes. Neither does it encourage the cyclist, who is faced with unnecessary legal restrictions. For example, it seems that the law will not protect a cyclist wheeling a bicycle across any type of pedestrian crossing, because this would technically amount to driving a vehicle across it. This means that it is not possible to design junctions for cyclists to cross busy main roads under the same traffic light arrangements as pedestrians. However, the law concerning the rights of cyclists on pedestrian crossings is by no means clear, and although a recent case at Stafford Magistrates Court indicates that protection is not given to a cyclist wheeling a bicycle across such crossings, recent government circulars[14] suggest the reverse.

It may be possible to simplify the existing law by making amendments to the relevant pieces of legislation, both to clarify points which are currently obscure and to change legislation which positively discourages bicycle planning. For example, granting Highway Authorities express statutory power to construct bicycle parking racks in the highway (see Chapter 7.7) would make a substantial difference. In addition to making small amendments, more radical changes should be considered; for example, allowing cyclists on all footpaths and footways except where specific prevention is required.

Alternatively, a long-term approach might be to create a new category of vehicle in law called 'the bicycle',[15] which would have to obey the relevant parts of vehicle law whilst being cycled or scooted and pedestrian law when being pushed. This approach would increase the freedom of the cyclist by recognising the essential differences between bicycles and other (motorised) vehicles, but would need to be carefully undertaken to ensure that it did not result in new restrictions being placed on the cyclist. To obtain a satisfactory result, considerable discussion between cycling organisations, local authorities, the police and the government will be necessary. However, a new bicycle bill would provide an opportunity to give cyclists the freedom to:

---

[14] Welsh Office Circular 108/76, para 14 and DOE Traffic Advisory Unit report, 'Provision for Cyclists', Nov. 1975.

[15] Clearly, the problems of tricycles and bicycles with trailers would have to be considered carefully before any final commitment was made.

Travel on all highways (except on motorways and other roads designated for special uses)

Travel on all footpaths

Push their bicycles anywhere, and be treated as a pedestrian rather than a vehicle when doing so

Park anywhere provided it does not cause serious obstruction.

Considerable research will be required to determine which approach would provide the greatest encouragement to planners and benefit to cyclists. We believe that central government has a responsibility to undertake this as a matter of priority because the requirements of current transport policy, which expects local authorities to submit proposals for cycling facilities, will be hard to satisfy within the current legal framework which seriously restricts the options available to planners.

5/The state of bicycle planning abroad

5.1 General introduction

The planning of transport facilities is one of those fields in which practice is at least as important as theory. The introduction of a new idea can be immeasurably assisted if reference can be made to actual examples elsewhere which are working satisfactorily. For example, before pedestrianisation was first introduced to this country (in Kings Lynn and Norwich in 1965 and 1967) visits had been made by both politicians and technical officers to see the continental examples that were then in existence.

The purpose of this chapter is to give some background information on bicycle planning in the towns and cities of other countries around the world. Emphasis is placed on specific examples, rather than on generalities, in the hope that where similar techniques are advocated for particular sites in the UK, the appropriate examples can be cited in support. It is probably true to say that there are examples, in other European countries alone, of every type of facility that might be considered for use in the UK. Although we have the Stevenage cycleway network, there are nonetheless many types and facilities which have not been tried here.

It is not easy, however, to argue that what works in one country will always work in another. There may be differences in social attitudes, economic activity and many other factors which conspire against a successful transplant. In China, for example, the bicycle takes the premier position as a mode of urban and rural transport. This is in keeping with their land-use patterns, social and political attitudes and economic priorities. The situation in the UK is so different as to make comparison fruitless except, perhaps, in the very longest of time scales. Even the Americans approach bicycle use in ways which cannot satisfactorily be compared with British practice. Their land-use patterns are not suited for cycling to be a significant mode of urban transport. Instead, it has a much greater role to play in recreation. As a consequence, the majority of the examples presented in this chapter come from continental countries, thus minimising the difference between the British situation and that found in the country used as an example.

The basic differences in approaching the problem in these countries results from the rigidity or flexibility of the design standards[1] which have to be applied. With the exception of Germany, the examples discussed in this chapter demonstrate the advantages of giving design guidelines which are advisory and which give as much scope as possible to the designer. The design guides which have been published in the countries discussed try to show a whole range of different ways in which the same problem can be tackled. The final solutions have depended on local knowledge and circumstances.

A similar philosophy has been developed in the United States. Their general philosophy has been summed up as follows:

> The standards provide guidance as to how the existing road system may be supplemented with facilities specifically designed to enhance the safety and feasibility of bicycle travel. The standards represent an attempt at a consensus as to what is required to provide a good level of service for cyclists. Since experience and research in this area are relatively limited, the standards are based on a combination of theory, empirical analysis, and the subjective judgement of cyclists.
>
> (*Highway Design Manual*, California Dept of Transportation, July 1974)

This honest and open approach to design standards has much to commend itself, and has now been adopted by the Federal Highway Administration. It is the type of approach which would be suitable for this country, where we have little experience in the provision of cycling facilities and where the lack of coordinated design of our towns and cities magnifies the problems of creating such facilities.

In this chapter we look at three examples, Sweden, Holland and Germany, to give a broad outline of the different approaches adopted on the continent. We then look, in more detail, at four specific problem areas: junction control; mixing cyclists and pedestrians; inner city traffic management; and countryside recreation routes. Solutions to these problems are essential to our basic thesis, and we draw extensively on continental experience in Chapter 7.

---

[1] The advantages and disadvantages of specific design standards are discussed in detail in Chapter 7.3.

The final section of this chapter looks at one example which is particularly successful, to show what can be achieved when a town is redesigned for bicycles.

5.2 Three examples of approaches in European countries

(i) *Sweden*

In 1973 the Swedish parliament asked for an investigation into how conditions for cyclists could be improved. This study was carried out and incorporated within a broader project laying down new guidelines for the planning of urban transport. The report[2] on bicycles deals with network planning, combining bicycles with pedestrians, buses and mopeds, law, junction design, signing, and the building of cycle routes. It was primarily intended as an aid to local authorities who are planning measures to assist cyclists.

The guide adopts a very flexible approach to network planning. It recognises that a cycle route network may consist of any of the following: (1) high standard, purpose-designed pedestrian and bicycle paths in the newly-built suburban areas of the town; (2) streets which carry a low volume of motor traffic and could also carry cyclists; (3) shared pavements, footpaths and pedestrianised streets. Stress is laid on the idea that where streets are widened, new roads built, or traffic management is introduced, cycle lanes or cycle tracks should be incorporated in the plan.

The design manual makes detailed regulations for signing and road marking, but the rest of the specifications are primarily advisory. It also gives a great deal of additional information about topics such as laws and traffic regulations, while providing general encouragement to local authorities to carry out studies of their area and to prepare plans for cycle routes.

---

[2] Some useful figures about bicycle use are given in this report. For example, 20 per cent to 30 per cent of all adults, and about 90 per cent of those age 7-17, cycle daily, or almost daily, during the summer months. Nonetheless, bicycle use in the 1970s is below the levels of the early 1960s, although bicycle sales have boomed in the 1970s. Bicycles and mopeds are used, on average, for 30 per cent of journeys to work (moped use is one-third of the level of bicycle use). Although levels of use during the cold Swedish winter fall to between one-half and one-tenth of the summer levels, it can be seen that cycling is still a relatively popular mode of transport, in spite of an extremely high level of car ownership. This is one of the reasons for their government's renewed interest in cycling.

One important principle behind the Swedish approach is that pedestrians, cyclists, and moped riders should, for the most part, have a common network.

A further principle of the Swedish Design Manual is the concept of progressive improvement of cycle routes. Having identified a route, priority is given to improving the most hazardous sections. Such an approach would be applicable to the UK, where the five-year rolling

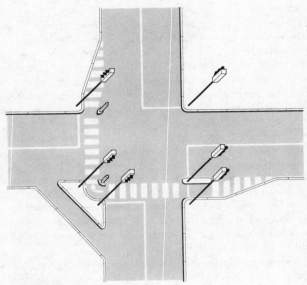

Figure 5.1   A two-stage junction.

programmes in the Transport Policies and Programmes are particularly suited to implementation by an on-going series of measures.

For cyclists in Sweden, there are two accepted measures of negotiating right turns at signalised junctions.[3] The first is to ride in the right turning lane and the second is to keep to the extreme left and to pull up in front of the waiting traffic in the next arm of the junction – then proceeding when the traffic in that arm is given the go-ahead. At some junctions, one or other of these movements only may be permitted, and the Swedes use a zebra-type road marking to delineate

[3] We assume, for the sake of clarity, that vehicles drive on the left hand side of the road.

the acceptable movement (see Fig. 5.1). These movements may, or may not, be controlled by small traffic signals directed specifically at the cyclists.

In other situations, where a cycle–pedestrian path approaches a road intersection, cyclists and pedestrians are treated together, both crossing at the same time on a combined cycle–pedestrian phase (Fig. 5.2). This is much like crossings in the UK, where a pedestrian phase

Figure 5.2 SWEDEN: New cycle route crossing a minor road. Note combined pedestrian–cycle use of footpath and separate lights for each mode.

has been incorporated in the overall signal cycle. At uncontrolled crossings, the path for cyclists is often marked out and signs warning approaching motor traffic of the potential hazard are erected.

(ii) *Holland*

Although Holland has the reputation of being a cycling country, bicycle use has dropped by 40 per cent since the 1950s and there are many gaps in the network of bicycle facilities, particularly in urban areas. Maps of existing facilities show clearly how cycle routes have been provided in outlying suburban areas and as part of post-war road and junction improvements in the inner areas, but not as part of a comprehensive network.

Holland has adopted a very different approach from Sweden. Traditionally, central government has provided little guidance or direction to local authorities. Advice has come from motoring and cycling organisations. In particular, 'Stichting Fiets' (the bicycle manufacturers' lobby organisation) has published pamphlets on the

Figure 5.3   HOLLAND: Experimental cycle route in The Hague. Note use of 'sleeping policeman' to warn cars attempting to turn off the main road across the cycle route.

need for, and method of, building cycle routes. As a result, local authorities have used their own standards to design bicycle facilities and have done very much as they wished. The only significant central coordination has been in the preparation of a nationwide network of long-distance routes.

In the last few years, planners and engineers have begun to take an increasing interest in cycling. A number of cities, including Amsterdam and Rotterdam, have plans to make comprehensive improvements to their existing bicycle facilities. In 1976 the government singled out The Hague and Tilburg for special financial assistance and encouragement. In both cities the routes have been planned to run from one side of the city, through the town centre, to the other side, and the Tilburg route has recently come into operation.

The scale of these routes (see Fig. 5.3) is much bigger and more expensive than anything yet envisaged in this country. This is hardly surprising, given the scale of the problem. For example, near the central area of The Hague, one existing road, soon to be converted to a joint cycle route and road, carries, in the peak hour, 4,500 cyclists, 2,500 mopeds and 1,000 cars.

It would be difficult to imagine the scale of congestion that would occur if even half of the cyclists and moped riders chose to make the same journey by car!

The cycle route in The Hague is some 10 kilometres long. Wherever possible, one lane of the existing road is going to be replaced with a two-way cycle route. Access to side streets is permitted but cyclists are protected by sleeping policemen where cars have to cross the cycle route. Where the street is wide enough, two-way motor traffic and parking is being retained. Where it is narrower, the street will be converted to one-way only for motor vehicles. Traffic signal control is used where the route crosses major roads.

In spite of the scale of the scheme, the planning of this route displays many of the principles which we believe are appropriate to this country. For example, one section of the route runs through a park and other sections use the back streets which run parallel to the main roads.

(iii) Germany

Apart from the apparent readiness with which cyclists and pedestrians are mixed, the German cycle routes are of interest because their design standards have been so extensively followed in towns and cities throughout the country. Whilst not every town or city can boast of such an extensive network as Hamburg or Münster, almost all have done something for the cyclists – along the recommended lines. The result of this approach is that bicycle facilities are readily recognisable anywhere in the country, but this has been at the expense of opportunities for local experimentation.

The German cycle routes basically consist of a 1·0 m-2·0 m wide strip in the pavement (Fig. 5.4), differentiated by colour or surface

Figure 5.4 GERMANY: Combined use of pedestrian facilities typical of the whole of Germany. Note the narrowness of the strip set aside for cyclists.

Figure 5.5 GERMANY: Cycle route at a major road junction in Hamburg. Note the carriageway markings which are both simple and cheap.

texture from the pedestrian area. Most of their bicycle routes are one-way, although there is often two-way utilisation of subways and wider paths. The use of dashed lines at road crossings is common-place (Fig. 5.5), as is the use of 'bicycle' and 'bicycle–pedestrian' signs, both of which serve to reinforce the motorist's awareness of the existence of cyclists.

Having discussed the general approach to cycle route design abroad, we now look in more detail at their approach to four particular areas of bicycle planning.

5.3 Junction control

Many countries on the continent have signal-controlled intersections which include special facilities for cyclists. Typically, cyclists are catered for with pedestrians, being controlled by the same set of lights and using adjacent pathways across the junctions.

Generally, Europeans mark out the route to be used by cyclists. The German form of a pair of dashed lines works well. The Danes do not at the moment mark out routes through junctions, mainly because the authorities do not have the necessary powers. Most countries have post-mounted push-button activation of the bicycle–pedestrian phase (as is found in the UK for pedestrian only phases). Induction loop activation of traffic lights has also been proved to be feasible but cannot, of course, be of use to pedestrians.

Unsignalled crossings present greater problems. Typically, where a bicycle route crosses a road at right-angles, it is necessary to warn both motor traffic and cyclists and perhaps reduce their respective speeds. The Swedes have an advantage here, because the zebra-type stripes present a readily recognisable warning to the motorist which is much more effective than simple triangular warning signs. There is little use of speed humps, width restrictions or chicanes to control the speed of motor vehicles by physical means, possibly because they would be counter-productive, diverting drivers' attention from the actual bicycle crossing. On the other hand, barriers, short uphill inclines, sharp bends and high kerbs are all used to discourage cyclists from speeding on the approaches to an unsignalised intersection. Such measures are in the interest of safer cycling and have the great advantage of being self-enforcing.

5.4 Mixing cyclists and pedestrians

This is an important subject, for there is a noticeable difference between the way cyclists and pedestrians are treated in the UK compared with the continental approach. It is rare in continental countries, for example, to see signs prohibiting cycling on pedestrian footpaths which can serve as short cuts. All too often such useful routes are banned in Britain.

The situation in the Scandinavian countries provides the best example. The Swedish Design Manual rules that where roadside parking is allowed a 3 metre pavement can readily be converted for joint pedestrian and bicycle use, and if there is no parking, 2·5 metres is the appropriate standard (the 0·5 metre difference allows for car doors to open). It is accepted that where bicycle and pedestrian flows are low, narrower pavements may be used. Such arrangements are working entirely satisfactorily in Västerås, Uppsala, Stockholm, Copenhagen, and many other places. It even works where there are shops and houses fronting directly on to the pavement.

In Västerås, in Sweden, a cycle route runs right through a pedestrianised city centre. This provides a good indication of the ease with which even heavy flows of cyclists and pedestrians can be mixed. The streets are not wide (7 m to 9 m), and shop fronts extend down either side. The cycle route is differentiated from the pavement by a change in the surface texture (but not by kerbs) and some delineation of the pedestrian area is achieved by the use of seats, trees and cycle parking racks (all fully used). No difficulties appear to have arisen with this approach.

The Dutch, in contrast to the Scandinavians, have always had to live with a much greater number of cyclists. As a result, much use has been made of footways – and many paths, instead of being banned to cyclists, are banned to pedestrians (particularly on rural cycle routes used for recreation). Nonetheless, the planning of cycle routes and facilities goes hand in hand with planning for pedestrians. It is therefore rare to see expensive facilities, such as an underpass or overbridge, which have not been designed with both users in mind.

The Germans, as we have already seen, make great use of footways. Designated bicycle paths are marked on footways which may be only 3 metres wide. Although such bicycle tracks are designed for one-way bicycle traffic, it is obviously not easy to stick to a one metre wide strip, for, if nothing else, pedestrians tend to wander over it regardless of the consequences. But as both cyclist and pedestrian are used to this situation, no major problems are experienced. Teenage cyclists present a little difficulty when they behave inconsiderately but no more than when they – and all other cyclists – are banned from footways, as in the UK.

5.5 Inner city traffic management

Catering for cyclists in the heart of city centres poses great problems. But it is in the heart of cities that there is most need to provide for cyclists and to make cycling both safer and more attractive than the use of a heavily congested road and public transport system. We have chosen as examples two cities where inner city traffic management has been used to the benefit of cyclists (as well as other groups in the community).

Stockholm (population: $1\frac{1}{2}$ million) has adopted a policy of creating environmental areas from which through traffic has largely been excluded. In the bicycle plan for the city, which was published in April 1975, this policy was chosen as the starting point for the city centre proposals. The cycle routes run through these environmental areas and all road closures now include a gap for the passage of cyclists.

Both temporary and permanent methods of road closure are used (see Fig. 5.6). The temporary closure is achieved with simple concrete blocks, pegged down to the road surface, and with appropriate gaps to allow cyclists to pass. The permanent closure involves an extension of the pavement across the width of the street. A short strip of this extended pavement is given a different surface treatment and aligned with the level of the carriageway. In this way, cyclists are able to ride through parts of the city centre on relatively quiet, lightly trafficked roads avoiding, whenever possible, the major intersections. It is admitted, however, that it is impossible to offer cyclists routes that avoid all major junctions. The plan therefore recommends that further measures to improve conditions for cyclists should be applied chiefly at major junctions.

The other example of inner city traffic management comes from Copenhagen. The Danes have approached the problem from a very different direction, but arrived at a solution which has remarkable similarities to the Swedish solution. The Danes' interest in the problem arose because they became seriously disturbed by the high accident rates for both cyclists and pedestrians that occur in most inner city areas. Østerbro was chosen for detailed study by a multi-disciplinary team. The end result was a series of traffic management proposals designed to give priority to pedestrians and cyclists. Simple techniques, such as sleeping policemen, road closures and narrowings, pavement extensions (designed so as to

Figure 5.6   SWEDEN: Typical road closures in central Stockholm – a permanent closure in the foreground and temporary closure behind.

increase sight-lines, thus improving pedestrian safety), and some bicycle lanes were specified and implemented.

The bicycle lanes run down the main spine road for the area, and through-traffic has been excluded from this route. The lanes have been positioned so that there are parked cars between the cyclist and moving traffic. The lanes are also wide enough to allow space to avoid car doors being opened in the way of oncoming cyclists.

Assessment of either the Danish or Swedish schemes is not easy, because improvements for cyclists are only a small part of the overall benefits that are sought. Nonetheless, both schemes do illustrate how it is possible, even in the congested centres of cities, to provide useful and attractive facilities for cyclists.

5.6 Countryside recreation routes

Cycle routes in the countryside designed for recreational use are common in Holland, are found on the fringes of many towns and cities in Germany, and have begun to be developed in Denmark.

The Danish example was planned by the county authority for Frederiksborg (the northern part of the island on which Copenhagen lies) and has been slowly implemented over the last few years. The basic path is rather like a well-surfaced bridleway (e.g. as in the New Forest) running through selected forests and other areas of attractive countryside, connecting inland places of interest – castles, museums – with the coastal resorts. These attractions are well signed and publicised along the route.

Where possible the routes are given a dual or triple purpose. They link in with schools and places of employment, so that commuters and school children also benefit. There has also been close liaison with the local railway company, who operate a bicycle 'hire-it-here, leave-it-there' policy at each of those stations up and down the line which runs close to one of the routes. The county authorities are pleased with the cycle routes which are being copied in other areas of Denmark.

In the German countryside there are many parks which have a network of cycle routes. The German railways also offer an extensive bicycle hire service at suburban stations.

The Dutch have adopted a rather different approach, and have opened up extensive areas of the countryside for cyclists, by using farm tracks, canal towpaths (of which there are many), footpaths and quiet country lanes. The network is comprehensive and a country-wide map is available from tourist offices. It should be noted, however, that the Dutch have been prepared to accept quite rough surfaces for their cycle routes both in towns and in the countryside. The surface is often made of small bricks or tiles which can feel decidedly uncomfortable. Nonetheless, the routes are well used and more are being developed.

5.7 A goal for planners

Finally, we look at Delft (Holland), which is a particularly successful example, both aesthetically and practically (Figs. 5.7, 5.8). It encompasses many of the principles of sympathetic 'street manage-

Figures 5.7 and 5.8   HOLLAND: Typical environmental traffic management in residential streets in Delft. Note use of flower beds, bollards, etc to discourage drivers from speeding and using the roads for short-cuts and detours.

ment' which, if applied to the UK, would present many opportunities for constructing cycling facilities in the future.

The streets in the historic core of the city are most attractive; they are extremely narrow and frequently run beside canals. To the south of the centre, however, lies a residential area developed in the nineteenth century. Although the streets are generally that much wider, only those houses redeveloped in the latter part of the twentieth century have garages. It is in this area that the planners and architects in Delft have been developing their concept of 'street management'. Simply stated this is to give top priority to pedestrians, then to cyclists, and lastly to the private car.

In order to achieve this new balance in favour of the pedestrian, pavements have been abandoned; street surfaces have been deliberately roughened by the use of cobble or brick and by introducing humps in the road; obstacles to vehicle movement have been introduced in the form of small bollards, and trees and shrubs, both individually and in island groups; and the parking spaces for cars are themselves arranged to act as a deterrent to unnecessary traffic.

The early experiments in Delft were most popular and have led to demands for similar schemes to be extended to other parts of Holland. In the UK many of our backstreets could be landscaped in a similar fashion, but until we take a more positive and courageous approach in this country, anyone wishing to see what streets might be like in a really sympathetic environment will have to travel abroad.

6/Current provisions for cycling in the UK

6.1 Historical background

Cyclists in the UK benefited dramatically from the tarmacadaming and asphalting of the dirt roads and tracks that were common well into the Edwardian era, but since then little else has been given to them from the public purse. During the inter-war years, cycling faced increasing regulation (i.e. compulsory lights and brakes) and efforts were made by the road engineers to remove cyclists from the new super highways that were then being planned and constructed and to put them on to cycle tracks alongside the dual carriageways. For a number of reasons, these cycle tracks were found to be of little benefit to cyclists:

(i) They seldom provided direct routes, since they were built alongside by-passes.
(ii) They were not integrated with other cycling facilities.
(iii) No provisions were made for cyclists at road junctions.

The tracks were frequently broken by driveways and service roads and were possibly more dangerous than the roads they were avoiding. It is therefore fortunate that few were constructed.

However, this 1930's concept of a cycle track persisted for many years. They were still being advocated in the government reports 'Roads in Urban Areas' (1966) and 'Roads in Rural Areas' (1968).

Another obstacle in the way of national bicycle planning was the method by which funds were provided for bicycle facilities. These were made available from highway funds, which could only be spent on highway land. Thus, although grants could be made by central government for the building of cycle tracks alongside trunk and principal roads, they could not be made for cycle routes which either followed a segregated pedestrian system or used the quieter back streets. This explains why the Stevenage cycleway system closely follows the main road system. This attitude prevailed until as recently

Figure 6.1   A cycle track in London.

as 1974, but has fortunately been rendered obsolete by the new
Transport Policies and Programmes system of giving grants for
transport investment.

With the significant exception of the new towns, the history of
bicycle planning in the UK up to 1970 can be summed up by saying
that there has been no conscious effort to plan for the use of the bicycle
which has produced concrete results. The 1970s have, however,
produced an upsurge of interest. After looking briefly at the new town
situation, the following sections will review Swindon, Bedford and
Portsmouth – these being the most interesting new developments in
existing towns.

6.2 Stevenage, Peterborough and other new towns

Before detailing the successful examples of Stevenage and Peterborough, it is important to set these two examples within the context

of the development of the new towns as a whole. None of the pre-Second World War garden cities, and only some of the post-war new towns, incorporated any special provision for bicycle facilities. For example, cycle tracks are absent from Hatfield, Hemel Hempstead, Runcorn and Warrington, but are present in Bracknell, Crawley and Harlow. It is advisable, however, to approach these latter examples with a certain scepticism. In most cases the network is incoherent and incomplete, and often inconsistent. In Crawley, for example, cyclists are allowed and indeed encouraged to share footpaths with pedestrians in certain areas – but not where this would be most desirable, in subways.

These examples come from some of the long-established new towns, where a substantial part of the planned development is already complete. In the 'younger' new towns, still at an early stage in their development, the situation is in many ways similar. Some have plans for cycle routes and others do not. In Milton Keynes, for example, cycle routes have been envisaged from the start. As a result, all subways have been built wide enough to accommodate pedestrians and cyclists, and the bicycle network is planned as an adjunct to the pedestrian network. This interest is particularly outstanding when it is remembered that Milton Keynes is probably our most car-orientated new town. In contrast, Runcorn, a new town where public transport has been given priority, has paid no attention to the problems of cyclists.

It is, then, fair to say that Peterborough and Stevenage, with their positive approach to bicycle planning, are exceptional among the new towns. The remaining twenty-eight have very little to show and the majority do not appear to have seized the opportunities provided by their 'green-field' sites.

Stevenage

The network of bicycle routes in Stevenage has been recognised as one of the best and most comprehensive in the world. There are about 23 miles (37 kilometres) of segregated routes, and about 90 subways. The cycleways are normally 3·5 metres wide and have footpaths of 2 metres next to them (see Fig. 6.2). The cycleways may be used by mopeds (up to 50 cc) and, for most of the system, they run beside the main roads. There are, however, some cross-town links created from what were originally country lanes.

The 1971 household survey showed that the 69,000 inhabitants owned 15,100 cars and 14,000 bicycles. Of these, 12,500 cars and 1,400 bicycles were used for the work journey. It should be emphasised that the car drivers have the use of an uncongested road network, even in the peak hours, and there is an excellent subsidised bus service. With such an excellent transport system, it is perhaps not surprising that only 9 per cent of the employed residents cycle to work, and 8·4 per cent of all children cycle to school (1971). However, this hides the fact that more secondary school age children cycle (17·4 per cent) than do primary school children.

Figure 6.2   The Stevenage cycle route network.

The existence of the cycleway system has given Stevenage an enviable safety record. Both cyclists and pedestrians share the benefits of the segregated system, which is virtually accident-free. There has never been a fatal accident on the pedestrian cycleway system, and, in the years to 1976, only 9 accidents involving cyclists and pedestrians have been reported. This approach has given Stevenage accident rates which are one-third of the national average.

Peterborough
Peterborough is an expanded new town in which a great deal has been done for cyclists, and more is planned. Unlike Stevenage, there was

already a large population in the city, some 80,000 in 1967, and the new development is being built around the existing settlement.

Cycle routes were planned in this new development from the very start and were incorporated in the 1971 Master Plan. An important feature of the planned network is that it runs directly from home to shops, schools and workplaces, thereby avoiding the main road network, which in most cases takes the less direct route around each

Figure 6.3   A segregated junction at Peterborough (photo from Peterborough Development Corporation).

area. This represents a significant improvement compared to the Stevenage situation.

Peterborough planners recognised that the pedestrian and bicycle networks could readily be combined. Indeed, new sections of the routes are simply three metre wide asphalt paths shared by both pedestrians and cyclists. On sections where flows are higher, a two metre strip is added and designated specifically for use by pedestrians. The strip has a slightly different surface marking and is raised a few inches above the level of the cycleway. Six metre wide subways are put in as often as finance will allow. Inevitably, given that there was an existing town before the new town was established, it has been necessary to consider ways in which the new town cycle routes could be extended right into the centre of the existing built-up area. This has posed rather more problems, partly because of the much more complex administrative and political set-up in the old town. Nonetheless, routes have been planned and the first experimental route was opened in July 1977 (see Fig. 6.3).

6.3 Provision in existing towns

Swindon

Turning to well established towns, one of the most interesting examples is provided by Swindon. Bicycle facilities have been steadily introduced into a number of areas of the town over the last few years. There are two major lengths of combined bicycle-pedestrian paths, one in a recent development, the other providing an exclusive bicycle-pedestrian crossing under the railway. Road closures have been made which exclude all vehicles except buses and cyclists and short sections of footpath and cycle track have been built to allow convenient short-cuts to be made by both cyclists and pedestrians. Special bicycle parking places have been established in the city centre. Finally, a cycle route plan has emerged as an integral part of a comprehensive transport plan.

The council have adopted a low-key approach, introducing bicycle facilities gradually and, whenever possible, combined in some way with either pedestrian or other traffic management measures. In themselves, none of the schemes has been large enough to stimulate a significant degree of public interest because people have not had to change substantially their travel habits. Consequently there has not been a focus of attention for public opposition, which has been minimal.

Another small detail has worked in the planners' favour in Swindon. The largest employer operates a car parking policy which actively promotes cycling. As the parking area within the factory is limited, spaces are only allocated to those who live more than two miles away. Employees who live nearby have to use public transport – which is far from adequate – or bicycle. This, surely, is an idea that other employers might follow in situations where their parking space is limited.

Bedford

Although Bedford is historically a cycling town, little has been done during the 1960s and early 1970s to provide facilities for the cyclist. Indeed a transport study carried out at the end of the 1960s totally ignored cycling. The five miles or so of pedestrian-cycle facilities that exist up to this date are mostly of pre-war origin.

In 1974 a new transportation study was begun. There are two features of this study which give it particular interest. Firstly, it was realised from the outset that bicycle use in Bedford was relatively high, and therefore information about bicycle use and ownership, as well as the usual information about trips by car, goods vehicle and public transport, was collected. Secondly, an extensive 'community involvement programme' was designed to seek the views of the public in developing alternative transport plans for the area.

The findings about bicycle use and ownership were startling. For example, it was discovered that residents owned more bicycles than cars. It was found that cycling was nearly as important as public transport, accounting for 14 per cent of all trips as against public transport's 16 per cent. Furthermore, it was not only the young who were cycling. The 45-64 year olds, for example, have a higher trip rate than the 15-25 year olds.

The community involvement programme was designed to give the study team a greater understanding of people's attitudes and travel behaviour. It aimed to reflect the ways people and groups perceived the existing transport system. The results showed universal endorsement of bicycle provision as being worthwhile to a large section of the population. People felt that it would not only be attractive to existing cyclists but would encourage others to join them. Children and older people in particular would gain from increased safety levels.

As a result, both the politicians and the professional officers have embraced cycling. The recommended plans have incorporated £650,000 worth of bicycle facilities and expenditure on the first parts has already started. This isolated example represents one of the most encouraging results to date in the UK.

Portsmouth

To turn to a town which has been less successful in providing facilities for cyclists, Portsmouth illustrates some of the practical and political difficulties of implementing such schemes. This town experimented with cycle routes for a period of seven months. Six kilometres of residential roads were designated as cycle routes, providing alternative parallel routes to busy main roads.

Briefly, the cycle routes consisted of the central three metres of carriageway, which were marked out as a cycle lane by two broken white lines and bicycle logos painted at intervals in this central section. On the cycle routes, motor traffic was prohibited except for access and residents' parking. Certain major junctions along the route were marked so as to give some priority to the cycle route and to

Figure 6.4   The Portsmouth cycle route network.

prevent motor vehicles from using the road as a through route (see Fig. 6.4).

The results of surveys taken during the experiment show that motor traffic on the routes was halved, but bicycle traffic increased by 15 per cent (elsewhere in Portsmouth the general level of bicycle traffic had decreased by 20 per cent). Of the one hundred cyclists interviewed who used the cycle routes, 4 had started cycling and 13 cycled more often because of the cycle routes. There were 52 cyclists unconditionally in favour of the routes, 32 liked the routes but objected to the motorists' behaviour, and 14 cyclists were against the scheme because they felt unsafe in the centre lane. It should be emphasised, however, that these observations are based on limited data and should be treated with some caution.

The experiment was terminated in the summer of 1976, mainly, it is understood, for political reasons – there being a local election in spring 1976. The cycle route was an issue because a minority of residents and local shopkeepers felt that they had been adversely affected by the scheme. There may be some justifications for these feelings as some residents may have had to make longer journeys to get to and from home. Other criticisms made of the cycle routes have more substance because they concerned faults in the design of the routes themselves.

Firstly, many motorists did not understand, or did not obey, some of the traffic directions. As a result, motor vehicles could be observed treating the junctions as mini roundabouts, or making a number of illegal movements around them. Other motorists ignored the 'no motor vehicles' signs[1] restricting traffic in certain roads, with the result that there were frequent examples of motorists driving in the bicycle lane and the wrong way up one-way streets.

Secondly, the cycle routes stopped some 20 metres before main roads and no special facilities were provided at crucial junctions. In addition, the routes were slightly less direct than the equivalent main roads.

Thirdly, the cycle routes were relatively expensive, at about £3,000 per kilometre. The heavy expenditure arose because of the extensive use of white lining and explanatory signs, which were necessary because of the design used to create the routes.

Nonetheless, these experimental cycle routes in Portsmouth have provided much useful experience, and the following lessons have been learned:

(i) as far as possible all bicycle priority measures should be self-enforcing;

(ii) they are best integrated with local environmental management schemes;

(iii) it is essential that facilities are also provided at points where the cycle routes cross main roads; and, finally,

(iv) there are advantages to encouraging cycling near the centre of the road, to increase the visibility of cyclists and to discourage motorists from pushing them unnecessarily into the kerb.

[1] See Chapter 7.6.

To summarise, then, in the UK there have been two important initiatives in the new towns, and three in existing towns. A number of other towns have undertaken minimal and only half-hearted steps to make provisions for cyclists, while all the rest have not done anything worthwhile. We therefore now move on to look in detail at the types of provisions which are appropriate to the UK.

7/Designing bicycle facilities

This chapter describes in detail the types of bicycle facilities which we think should be incorporated into many of the towns and cities of the UK. So far we have argued for the provision of facilities and described progress to date. This section of the report takes the constituent parts of a cycle route network and describes the possible solutions to particular problems and analyses their merits and drawbacks. Although each part of the design is treated separately here, the final design of the complete network should be carefully coordinated to ensure that each type of bicycle provision is compatible with the rest of the network.

7.1 The ideal conditions for cycling

Bicycle journeys in cities are generally taken to get to work, school or shops. Certain points must be taken into account when designing facilities for these journeys. In particular, cyclists will be reluctant to take a longer or harder route, even if it is safer, and secondly cyclists dislike having to slow down or stop frequently, because in doing so they lose momentum. Bearing these two points in mind, a list of ideal facilities for cyclists can be compiled:

(1) Routes should be direct and connect as many starting points and destinations as possible
(2) Routes should be free from heavy traffic
(3) Routes should be well signposted
(4) Provision should be made for the safety of cyclists at junctions. These should involve minimum delay for cyclists
(5) All other road users, including pedestrians, should be informed of, and expect to find, cyclists on the routes
(6) Routes should not involve unnecessary hill climbing
(7) Routes should be well surfaced

(8) Parking facilities should be provided at all destinations
(9) As far as possible, routes should be attractive – for example, running through parks
(10) Routes should avoid areas subject to extremes of climate, such as wind traps or snow and leaf traps
(11) Routes in open spaces should, where possible, be lit to avoid providing cover for vandals and muggers
(12) Routes should be designed to facilitate and minimise maintenance requirements.

In practice it would be very difficult to meet all these requirements and compromises will have to be made. However, a system designed for cyclists which satisfied these criteria would both encourage cycling and make it safer. The importance of being sensitive to the needs of cyclists cannot be over-emphasised. Unless this is done, facilities will be under-used and therefore harder to justify.

7.2 Different types of cycle route

The term CYCLE ROUTE has become widely accepted as a generic term. It is used to describe all the types of routes described below:

CYCLE TRACK   This term is used to describe the 3 metre paved tracks which were built alongside some major road constructions between the 1930s and 1950s, in an attempt to protect cyclists from the dangers of heavy traffic. Their failure has already been documented (see chapter 6) and was partially responsible for the lack of subsequent provisions.

CYCLEWAY   In Britain the term cycleway was introduced to describe the provision of independent cycle routes in new towns. These generally consist of tarmac strips which were sometimes constructed beside main roads, but more recently they were completely segregated from motor traffic.

CYCLE PATH   This is a paved strip which is always completely separated from motor traffic though it may be shared with pedestrians. Opportunities for providing cycle paths arise in large developments, within existing cities, on green field sites and also in some semi-rural situations, for example between a town and a neighbouring village.

CYCLE LANE   A cycle lane consists of a strip of roadway designed primarily for the use of cycles. It is similar to a bus lane but may be narrower and could be provided on any type of road. Cycle lanes are widely used in the USA and Holland, but in Britain combined bus and cycle lanes are more common. They are suitable in contra-flow situations to avoid the effects of one-way systems or in with-flow situations to give cyclists a clear run up to busy junctions without having to manoeuvre around stationary vehicles. They can either completely prohibit motor vehicles from entering the lane (by using a solid white line demarcation) or be advisory, requesting motorists to give cyclists protection whenever possible (denoted by a broken white line). However, since the bicycles and other vehicles are only segregated along uninterrupted routes, junctions remain a major hazard. In addition, a cycle lane is seldom a pleasant or attractive place for cycling but in urban situations where a main road is the most direct route it may be the only practical way of providing some protection for cyclists. Cycle lanes also provide the best solution where main roads cannot be avoided, for example on bridges.

It is essential that no vehicle parking or stopping be permitted on the cycle lane, and that the edge of the road is well maintained and gullies are made suitable for cycle traffic.

A number of types of lane demarcation, used to segregate cyclists from other vehicles, are currently available. These include: white lines, studs laid in the road, narrow paved strips (to create a noise) or a continuous raised hump. Long stretches of guard-railing cannot normally be used because it prevents access to private property and side streets. In some cases the provision of cycle lanes will require finding new road space. This may be achieved by restricting on-street parking or by reducing motor lane widths. The latter need not reduce road capacity since this is largely controlled by intersections. Another possibility is to reduce pavement widths or to share a pavement between pedestrians and cyclists.

CYCLE TRAIL   A cycle trail is a route for the use of cyclists – and possibly pedestrians – through parks, commons and other amenity areas. The trail may be designed for recreational use or as a part of a network for direct journeys. A cycle trail should generally be built to a standard similar to that for cycle paths, though a tarmac surface is not an essential prerequisite for such a route. The width will depend on whether the trail is shared with pedestrians or not. Ideally, it should be flat and completely separated from other traffic. The trail must be clearly marked, possibly by cycle symbols stencilled on the surface so that pedestrians expect cyclists. A disused railway, which cannot be brought back into service, is just one example of the many opportunities for providing cycle trails.

DESIGNATED CYCLE ROUTE   This is a route which is designed for cyclists, and motor traffic has limited access. Typically, this route is found within backstreet environmental areas.[1] It is likely to be the basic tool for adapting existing cities to provide networks of cycle routes. The maze of back street routes in our towns and cities presents many opportunities for encouraging cycling. The routes should be cleared of other traffic by placing ramps, gates or bollards across the road (see Chapter 7.5). Routes need not be stencilled throughout their length since this is itself an environmental intrusion. Rather, routes should be clearly marked to direct cyclists to their destinations (see Chapter 7.6). Junctions should give cyclists priority where flow-rates justify this, and should always give cyclists maximum protection from other traffic (see Chapter 7.4).

7.3 The application of design standards

Standards are rigid formulae applied to the construction of cycle routes (e.g. maximum gradients, tightest bends, road surfacing) and to the design of road markings and road signs.

The most obvious reason for having standards is to achieve a degree of uniformity throughout the country. The advantages of uniformity include ease of comprehension since people react almost instinctively to well-known features, such as the flashing beacon at zebra crossings. It is important that facilities for cyclists are readily recognisable and one of the best ways to achieve this is to use standard highway markings and signs.

The second reason for building cycle networks to defined standards is that they can be used to identify parts of a network or even whole towns where there are deficiencies. Financial, or indeed any, resources, can then be allocated in such a way as to bring the facilities 'up to standard'.

A final reason for setting standards is to improve safety. It may be necessary, for example, to ensure adequate visibility on the approaches to a particular type of junction if it is to operate safely.

[1] These are usually characterised by a large number of residential streets which run parallel to the main road network and have been closed to through traffic to improve the local environment. The proximity of local schools, the lack of play areas and the incidence of child road accidents, are also reasons for creating environmental areas.

Standards may even be developed further into legal requirements – e.g. red rear and white front lights on cycles – which have an important safety element. They may also be of consequence when any question of liability arises. Highway Authorities are noticeably reluctant to commit themselves to any scheme if there is the slightest chance that they may in some way be liable for claims that the scheme was not safe. If they work to established national standards, they will feel more protected.

However, there are a number of valid reasons against having standards. Perhaps most important is the danger of centrally imposed standards stifling local initiatives. Standards create bureaucratic obstacles which have to be overcome before a new, unconventional idea can be tried out in practice. Secondly, standards which may be applicable for the majority of situations may be quite inappropriate in a specific locality.

Another danger in setting standards is that when they are set too high they can make provisions prohibitively expensive and in some situations could make it impossible to provide for cyclists. For example, a standard for the maximum gradient of a cycle route set at 10 per cent would rule out a short section of cycle route of 12 per cent which cyclists could in fact push their bicycles up. Alternatively, if set too low, they will be of little value to the planner.

Finally, rigid standards may rule out an otherwise suitable route if one section falls below the specification. This might result in the provision of a generally less suitable route whose only merit was that it satisfied these standards.

It is our contention that, except in the areas of signing and road marking, the adoption of rigid standards in the UK would not be beneficial to the imaginative design of cycle networks.

However, for the purpose of practical design, and in particular for engineers who will need to know what size of provision will cater for certain conditions, it is necessary to give a perspective on both the optimum standards which provide first class cycling facilities and on absolute standards which provide a bare minimum of cycling facilities.

Optimum standards are suitable for new development sites and would provide the best encouragement for cycling. Absolute standards will, however, be more widely applicable for adapting existing sites. These are based on the maximum dimensions of a bicycle with an allowance for cyclists' 'wobble' and minimum clearances. The basic standards which should be kept in mind are an optimum minimum width for bicycles of 1·5 m and an absolute minimum of 0·8 m.

However, different types of cycle facilities require different widths; for example, the width of a cycle lane must ensure that parts of the bicycle or the cyclist never have to encroach on the main roadway,

Table 7.1   Widths for cycle routes[1]

	Optimum Standard (metres)	Absolute Standard (metres)
CYCLE LANES		
One way	2·00[2]	1·50
Two way	3·60	1·80
CYCLE DESIGNATED ROUTES		
Two way	4·00	2·00
Width between bollards	1·50	0·80
Width between bollards, allowing for tricycles[3]	–	1·53
CYCLE TRACKS AND TRAILS[4]		
One way (heavy traffic)	2·75	–
One way (light traffic)	2·00	1·20
Two way (heavy traffic)	3·60	–
Two way (light traffic)	3·00	1·60
Shared footpaths (Two way)	3·00[5]	1·60[6]

[1] These figures should be treated as guidelines. They have been produced as a best estimate of required widths, but there is nothing sacrosanct about them.
[2] Allows for overtaking on bus lanes.
[3] Motorcycles could pass through this gap.
[4] Clearances can overlap the trail edge thus reducing minimum widths.
[5] With dividing line.
[6] Light traffic and without dividing line.

whereas, on a cycle trail, which is free from fast moving traffic, tolerances need not be so large (Table 7.1).

The width of a cycle route also depends on the expected flow rates of bicycles, and Fig. 7.1 shows an approximate relationship between the width of a cycle route and its maximum capacity.

Gradients
The criteria for the maximum gradients of cycle routes should take into account the distance over which a particular gradient has to be

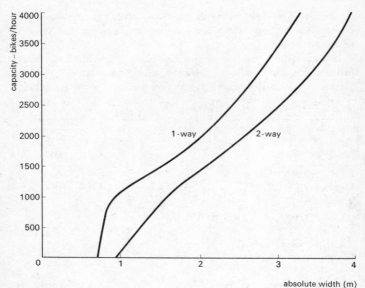

Figure 7.1   Cycle route capacities.

Source: Bikeways: the state of the art, 1974.

cycled. Furthermore, pushing cycles up steep unavoidable hills should not be discounted as unreasonable. Thus specifications for gradients consist of the set of curves (taken from Dutch experiments) shown in Fig. 7.2.

Radius

Speed is the main factor determining the minimum radius of curvature of a cycle route. The generally accepted formula[2] gives a radius of 6·3 m at an optimum speed of 25 kph. A curve of smaller radius should be signed as a sharp bend and where the radius is less than 2 m cyclists should be instructed to dismount. Normally, cycle routes should be designed with the largest possible radii, but on junction approaches it may be necessary to have smaller radii or steeper gradients to force cyclists to slow down.

[2] $R = 0·24V + 0·42$
R = radius in metres
V = speed in kilometres per hour.

Sightlines

A sightline is a line to the road side of which there is a completely unrestricted view. The length of a sightline is the distance from a vehicle (or bicycle) to another vehicle or pedestrian just coming into sight around a corner. (Fig. 7.3). These are most important on shared pedestrian-cycle routes and where the tolerances of a particular route are low. The Greater London Council recommend a minimum sightline of 10 m for cyclists on shared footpaths. The length of sightlines should also take into account the gradient of the approaches to a junction. On descending gradients of over 5 per cent increased sightlines are required because stopping distances for cyclists are greater when descending than when ascending.

Surfacing

All cycle facilities should be as smoothly surfaced as possible, as most bicycles do not have shock absorbing suspension. A smooth surface makes pedalling much easier. Furthermore, the surface should be maintained in a good condition. Potholes, even small ones, can cause severe damage to bicycle wheels and bicycle riders.

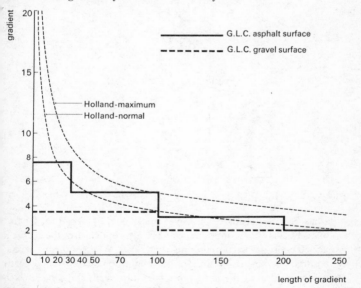

Figure 7.2 Maximum gradients for cycle routes.

Surfaces should preferably be mastic asphalt or dense tar, but concrete paving, paviors or even smooth hard bricks laid in cement mortar can be used. Cobbles and rough paving should be avoided. Cross falls of about 2·5 per cent should be provided in keeping with any curve in the cycle route.

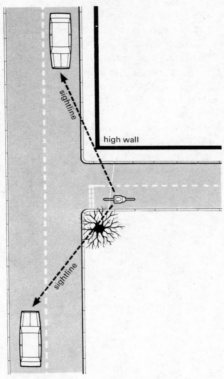

Figure 7.3   Sightlines.

It has been suggested that gravel tracks could be used for leisure cycling. This is not recommended as a large proportion of the cyclist's expended energy is used in moving the gravel. Where a cheap surface is required for leisure cycling, either hoggin or beaten rolled earth should be used with adequate cross falls to prevent standing surface water.

Lighting

Provisions for leisure cycling and provisions outside urban areas will rarely require lighting. In urban areas the standard should be similar to that provided on estate and minor roads.[3]

7.4 Junction design

The problem of designing junctions for the safe passage of bicycles and other vehicles has never been satisfactorily solved and today this is the most difficult problem facing the cycle route designer. The only solutions which have a good safety record are the new town networks, and these have adopted a policy of complete segregation of bicycles from other vehicles. Generally, this solution is not suitable for cycle route networks in existing towns and cities because of space and cost limitations.

Alternatives are therefore required which balance a number of conflicting requirements. Safety is the most important criterion since over 70 per cent of all cycle casualties in built-up areas occur at junctions. Ideally, since all stops mean extra work for cyclists, discontinuities in the cycle route should be avoided. However, these requirements have to be satisfied within cost limits which are proportional to the anticipated vehicle flows at a junction and within the constraints of the land available for re-designing the junction.

Finding solutions which satisfy these criteria will not be easy, and in an attempt to outline the possibilities and the situations in which these are suitable we consider the problems of traffic management measures at junctions, firstly on designated cycle routes, both at major and minor road junctions. We then consider junctions on routes exclusively for cyclists, again at major and minor junctions. Finally, we look at the possibilities at new construction sites and at some changes to junctions on ordinary roads which would make city cycling a much more attractive proposition.

Junctions on designated cycle routes

(i) **Junctions with major roads** We will explain later that motor vehicle flows should be below 100 for a designated cycle route to be successful. Where vehicle flows on the cycle route approach this figure and where they are above 1,100 vph on the main road, traffic

[3] British Standard Group B.1.

lights will provide the most suitable solution. To minimise the loss of road capacity on the main route they could be triggered by a loop detector in the designated cycle route. If pedestrian facilities were provided, a completely separate traffic light phase or banned turns would have to be introduced to avoid vehicles conflicting with pedestrians[4] (Fig. 7.4).

At staggered junctions where the stagger is small enough for motor vehicles turning into the major road to realise that they will be

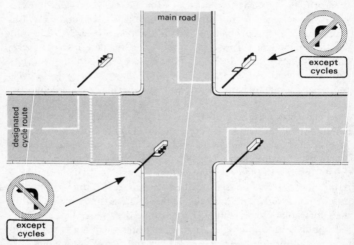

Figure 7.4   Designated cycle route crossing a main road.

crossing the path of those remaining on the designated route, traffic lights again provide the most suitable solution (Fig. 7.5).

Where the stagger is larger, the provision of two sets of traffic lights might be considered, but this is likely to be prohibitively expensive and there is a limit to the proximity of such sets[5] (Fig. 7.6).

Where the traffic flow on the main road is lower than 1,100 vph, a wide island (Fig. 7.7) could be provided to give cyclists protection. Clearly, right turns into and out of the designated cycle route would have to be banned to motor vehicles, but this might be advantageous in some situations since it will further control the number of vehicles

[4] Although the DTP have not officially accepted bicycles turning across pedestrians on the same phase, it is common practice in some places (e.g. Oxford Street, London).
[5] The DTP does not give a figure and considers each case on its own merits.

using the route. The island would also narrow the road and slow down traffic on the main road.

At a staggered junction, this island could be modified to form a sheep pen (Fig. 7.8) without losing the advantages of the island.

An alternative and substantially cheaper solution, if the vehicle flow-rate on the designated route is near the 100 vph limit and the flow-rate on the main road is only moderate, would be to provide a

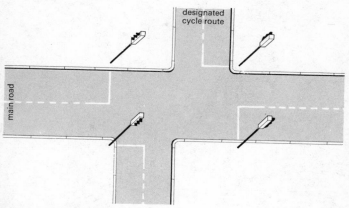

Figure 7.5 Staggered junction.

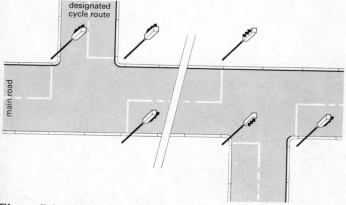

Figure 7.6 A long staggered junction.

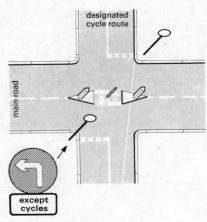

Figure 7.7 A wide island crossing.

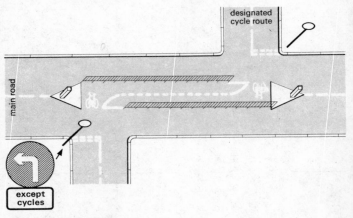

Figure 7.8 A sheep pen.

small roundabout. This has the added advantage of not greatly reducing the capacity of the main road. These roundabouts could be designed to present a solid obstacle which traffic would have to drive round at slow speed. They would also ensure that cyclists only had to cross one lane of traffic at a time (Fig. 7.9).

(ii) **At minor road junctions** Junctions between designated cycle routes and minor roads are likely to be prevalent where cycle routes pass through areas of dense residential road networks. In these situations the most useful device may be a simple priority change, with the appropriate signing. Where necessary the speed of other vehicles could be controlled by sharp road narrowing on each lane (Fig. 7.10).

Where traffic volume on the minor road is appreciable it might be possible to justify traffic lights, though expense is likely to limit the

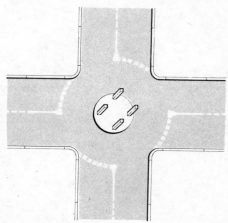

Figure 7.9 A small roundabout.

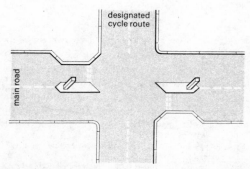

Figure 7.10 Sharp road narrowing.

use of these. Where vehicle flow on the designated cycle route is appreciable (100 vph) a small roundabout might provide a realistic solution.

Junctions on routes exclusively for cyclists
(i) **Junctions with major roads**   There are many situations where an exclusive cycle route will have to cross a busy main road, both within city centre areas, where cycle routes cannot avoid a dense network of major roads, and in outlying areas where radial cycleways cross major ring roads.

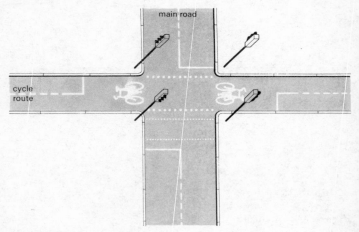

Figure 7.11   Exclusive cycle route crossing a main road.

Where the traffic volume on the major road is high, methods are required to stop the main traffic flow. Traffic lights will often provide an effective but expensive solution. Loop detectors[6] can be set in the cycle route to trigger the lights, and in many situations where traffic volumes are not large, the detectors can be positioned and tuned to change the lights as the cyclist arrives, thus avoiding unnecessary stops. The green light for cyclists[7] need only last for a few seconds,

[6] These are wire loops set in the road which detect the presence of a cyclist and trigger the relay which changes the lights.
[7] A green 'bicycle-logo' shine-through light is both legal and practical and could be incorporated into a smaller signal set for cyclists to avoid unnecessary visual clutter.

thus minimising delays to other traffic which might be tempted to violate a longer red light.

A pelican crossing could also be incorporated to change in phase with the cycle route, provided neither pedestrian nor bicycle flow rates are particularly high (Fig. 7.11). Cyclists should always be

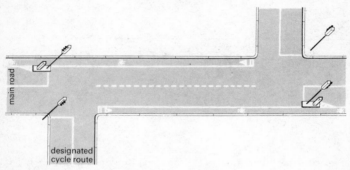

Figure 7.12 The right then left stagger.

informed that pedestrians are crossing and this can be achieved by ensuring that the pedestrian lights are clearly visible to cyclists.

Crossing major roads becomes slightly more complicated at junctions which are staggered. Two situations have to be considered – the 'left then right' stagger and the 'right then left' stagger. For relatively short staggers (say up to 25 m) where only one set of traffic lights are required, the right then left junction can be solved with two one-way cycle lanes. This configuration minimises delays to other vehicles, because they are only held up whilst the cyclists cross the road (Fig. 7.12).

However, two-way cycle lanes have to be used at longer staggers (see Figs. 7.13, 7.14) because there is a limit to the separation of one set of traffic lights. They will also have to be used at 'left then right' junctions. In both these situations fixed guardrailing will be required to segregate cyclists from on-coming traffic, so the main road will have to be more than 10 m wide, because the guardrailing, with minimum tolerances, takes up 1 m. Again, pelican crossing facilities could be added in both situations provided that cyclists were aware that pedestrians were crossing on the same phase.

Where traffic flows are below 800 vph, other cheaper solutions will be more suitable. For example, at a straight junction a wide island could be provided in the middle of the road to break the crossing of the road into two parts (Fig. 7.7). The island would also act as a road-narrowing and slow traffic down at the junction. Alternatively,

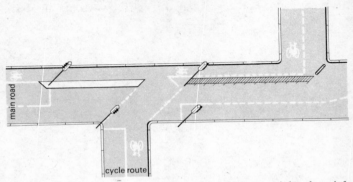

Figure 7.13 Two-way cycle lane solution to a right then left staggered junction.

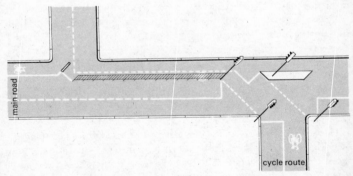

Figure 7.14 Two-way cycle lane solution to a left then right staggered junction.

at a staggered junction, a sheep pen could be provided to give cyclists extra protection (Fig. 7.8).

Where an exclusive cycle route joins the main road at a T-junction, cyclists can be given priority by making the junction into a cross roads. Careful positioning of the loop detectors will ensure that cyclists do not have to stop, but that they are slowed down before they reach the junction (Fig. 7.15). (This design is used in Peterborough.)

(ii) **Minor junctions**   The problems of exclusive cycle routes crossing minor road junctions are not as acute as those at major junctions and are not likely to occur nearly as frequently as minor junctions on designated cycle routes. The problems may be found

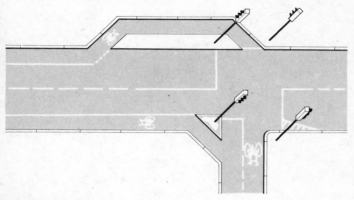

Figure 7.15   T-junction.

where newly constructed cycle routes have to cross minor roads in outlying areas.

Sometimes a simple priority change, giving cyclists priority over other vehicles, will be all that is required. However, if bicycle flow-rates are low, drivers will tend not to expect cyclists and will thus drive straight over the junction without waiting. The DTp road markings[8] and the standard cycle warning signs[9] can be used to give drivers maximum warning, and, where cycle and vehicle flow rates justify it, small roundabouts can be used to present a solid obstacle to drivers.[10]

Generally in these situations traffic lights or islands and guardrailing will not be justifiable and if traffic flows are appreciable then

[8] See Chapter 7·6.

[9] See Chapter 7.6.

[10] Although this looks a relatively straightforward matter, we have not found any examples where the DTP has allowed these measures to be introduced.

cyclists may just have to wait at some junctions and be given priority at others.

New construction sites
New developments present planners with opportunities to create first class cycling facilities. It will sometimes be possible to provide cycling facilities which are completely segregated from other traffic. But more

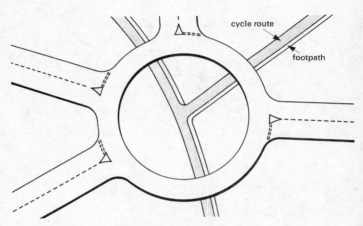

Figure 7.16 A grade separated junction.

often joint cycle-pedestrian facilities will avoid unnecessary expenditure whilst remaining completely safe.

Two situations require consideration:

(a) ON NEW HOUSING ESTATES it will usually be possible to provide completely segregated cycle routes, but complete segregation at junctions will sometimes not be justifiable because traffic flows are generally quite low. Large central islands (Fig. 7.7) or small roundabouts could be used to give cyclists protection. Where flows are very low it will not be necessary to provide any facilities and where they are higher (for example on the perimeter roads of an estate) the provision of traffic lights might be justified. The same principles should be used when redesigning substantial areas of housing in existing urban areas.

(b) When DESIGNING NEW TOWNS planners should aim to provide completely segregated facilities. All major junctions could be grade separated and minor ones could have islands and small roundabouts. Complete segregation was the principle behind the Stevenage network which has now become world famous (Fig. 7.16).

Junctions on ordinary roads

We have already explained that the problems at junctions present the greatest dangers to cyclists. There are many situations where careful design of junctions which are not necessarily part of an overall cycle route network could considerably improve both the safety and the waiting time for cyclists.

It is essential that local authorities examine and consider the potential for improving the design for cyclists when redesigning junctions for traffic management purposes. Indeed we believe that local authorities should examine all junctions to see if modifications would be feasible. Each junction must be considered as a unique case, but below we list some possible modifications which would be applicable to many junctions.

At junctions which are controlled by traffic lights, the cyclist making a right turn or crossing over the junction will in general have to wait, with cars, for a green light. However, there will be some situations at busy junctions where a green shine-through cycle light should be used to give cyclists a few seconds start over cars, enabling them to make both right and straight across movements before the car lights turn 'red and amber'. One design would be to place a cycle light low on the traffic signal post to avoid confusing other drivers. When the green cycle light is not lit, cyclists will have to obey the ordinary traffic signals.

Provisions for left-turning cyclists may be more easy to justify since they need not hold up motor traffic. High priority should however be given to pedestrians' safety and cyclists' speed must be carefully controlled. Measures allowing the cyclist to use the footway will only be possible where there is considerable space available on the pavement (Fig. 7.17). Where one-way systems force traffic to make left turns a higher proportion of cyclists using the junction will be catered for.

At T-junctions controlled by traffic lights more substantial provision can be made for cyclists. This arrangement allows half of the cyclists using the junction to cross without having to wait at traffic lights, and motor traffic is not held up at all (Fig. 7.18).

At very busy urban junctions it will often be possible to introduce stretches of cycle lane to give cyclists a clear run up to all types of junction so that they do not have to weave through stationary traffic. A loop detector set in the cycle lane could be used to trigger the cycle light. Extensive use of this sort of provision would make city centre cycling a much more attractive means of transport.

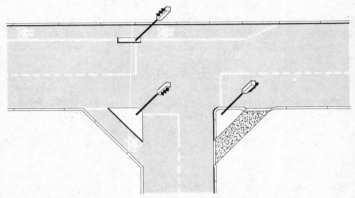

Figure 7.17   Provision for left-turning cyclists.
and
Figure 7.18   Cycle lane to avoid delays to cyclists at a T-junction.

7.5 Keeping traffic out of designated cycle routes

Introduction
It has already been explained that designated cycle routes will play an important part in the provision of overall cycle networks (Chapter 7.2). Ideally, access should be limited to residents and delivery vehicles. These routes are only valuable to cyclists if the traffic flow is less than a maximum of about 100 vehicles per hour. Below this figure, cycling will be both pleasant and safe, car-owning residents are not likely to protest about lack of access to their homes, and these and other residents will appreciate the quieter environment. Above about 100 vehicles per hour, cyclists will be increasingly discouraged and the route will cease to be an attractive alternative to other streets.

Both pedestrians and the vehicles using the routes should be made aware of the presence of cyclists and warned to give them priority. This will require careful signing, both to clearly inform these other two categories of road users and to ensure that cyclists are aware that they have been informed. This will give cyclists confidence and encourage them to use the routes. Before a designated cycle route is created, the nature of the traffic on the existing route will have to be determined; if it is primarily commuter traffic using the route as a 'rat run', then traffic restraint is more justifiable than if the traffic is primarily residential, when restraint will only annoy local residents.

The type of area in which this kind of measure is most appropriate usually consists of a network of backstreets, so keeping traffic out of one road will only put pressure on another unless the road that is closed is the only clear, straight road through the area. Thus designated cycle routes frequently have to be considered as part of an overall traffic and environmental plan. Further measures to minimise interference to local residents include the careful positioning of barriers, since some types of experimental barriers are unsightly. These barriers will often only be temporary and can later be replaced by permanent features which are more attractive.

Barriers across roads chosen for cycle routes fall into two broad categories: passable and impassable. Impassable barriers are easier to implement, both legally and physically, whilst passable barriers are still to a great extent experimental.

Impassable barriers
Although these are sometimes completely impassable, access frequently has to be provided for emergency vehicles. The two ways of creating barriers which give such access are 'knock-down' or 'lift-out' bollards. These are quite easy for local authorities to implement using the Road Traffic Regulations Act 1967 s. 1, s. 5 and s. 6; or s. 9 for experimental schemes. In addition s. 69 and s. 70 give authorities power to place obstructions in the highway where orders are made according to s. 1, which defines the reasons for making such orders. In situations where emergency access is not required, roads could be closed by creating footpaths or bridleways under the Highway Act 1959 s. 28, but the existing highway would have to be diverted, using s. 108. Where large-scale planning is being undertaken, for example the creation of pedestrian precincts, s. 212 of the Town and Country Planning Act 1971 will be appropriate.

There are no major problems in allowing bicycles to pass through road closures; for example, it is now the policy of the Greater London Council to exempt bicycles from road closures made on environmental grounds (i.e. not in 'stopping up' orders at main roads). The gaps for cyclists should be 0·8 m wide to allow cyclists to pass easily without allowing motorcycles through, and they should be clearly signed (see Chapter 7.6). The sign need not be illuminated in temporary schemes, and possibly not in permanent ones, and can be mounted on the bollards which form the road closure, to reduce cost and eliminate visual clutter.

Passable barriers (throttles)
As a result of opposition to permanent barriers from local car-owning residents, increasing attention has been paid to passable barriers. Although there will always be a percentage of vehicles violating the 'access only' sign, one or a combination of the measures described will bring vehicle flows down to the target figure of 100 vehicles per hour. However, it is worth noting that this is a relatively untried area so it is difficult to give hard and fast rules.

(i) **Access ramps**   Under s. 212 of the Town and Country Planning Act the footway can be extended across the mouth of the road at a junction (Fig. 7.19). This is a useful device since most drivers are deterred by having to drive over the pavement, which could be differentiated by using a different colour of paving slabs.

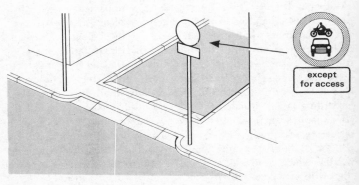

Figure 7.19   An access ramp.

However, there have not been any opportunities for the Secretary of State to allow such a ramp away from a junction. The principle of the ramp is that the road is closed 'except for access', but to date, absence of a legal definition of 'access' has prevented widespread use of this device. Permission from the DTp to use terms such as 'except for residents and deliveries' would make more widespread use both possible and practical.

Further discouragement to drivers could be provided by reconsidering the concept of a street. At present most residential streets are straight and built to high standards with lengthy sightlines, well defined kerbs and wide pavements. This encourages cars to take short cuts and travel at 30 mph.

An alternative to this traditional attitude, which is already being considered by the DOE[11] and put into practice in Sheffield,[12] is to design or alter streets to give them a sense of place, with less formal road layouts. This would be done by making the carriageway narrower and adding attractive street furniture, for example benches, garages, shrubs or trees, to provide restricted sightlines and tight bends to deter motor vehicles. At the entrances to such streets ramps would be constructed to present a psychological barrier to drivers and to reduce the speed at which they can drive in comfort. There would be no differentiation between the road and the pavement, so the driver would be made to realise that he is driving in a community area. Grassing over the area on both sides of the road, or introducing cobbles or other textural alterations, are further possibilities. Although this type of attention would be costly, it certainly would stop or slow down all through traffic and enhance the local environment (see photos of Delft, Figs 5.7, 5.8).

(ii) **Road narrowing** Access ramps will be more effective when used in conjunction with other throttles. Under the Highway Act 1959, s. 5 powers exist to vary the relative widths of the carriageway and footway and of cycle tracks. Used on its own, this will slow down vehicles but it will allow flows of up to 1,000 vph. To give cyclists priority and protection, gaps on either side of the narrowing should be provided (Fig. 7.20). These could also be arranged in the form of a chicane and could be used to restrict access to long heavy lorries (Fig. 7.21).

[11] See 'Access Roads in Residential Areas', DOE, July 1977.
[12] See *Surveyor*, 3 June 1977.

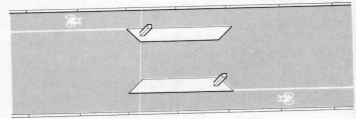

Figure 7.20 A road narrowing.

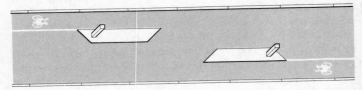

Figure 7.21 A chicane.

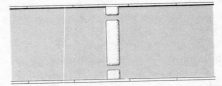

Figure 7.22 Road hump with a valley for cyclists.

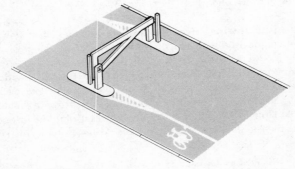

Figure 7.23 A soft-faced gate.

(iii) **Road humps (sleeping policemen)** These were included in the 1974 Highways Act for introduction on a 12-month experimental basis. They cannot be placed on main roads and must be authorised by the DTp. Results from the experimental humps at Oxford show that they successfully achieve the aim of slowing down traffic. The humps have to be of a specified height, width and frequency and must be signed 'Humps for n miles' to exempt the highway authority from damages caused to vehicles.

So far no road hump has been designed to cater for cyclists, but it would be relatively simple to make gently sloping valleys in the hump to allow cyclists an easy passage. There would be no need for additional signposting (Fig. 7.22).

(iv) **Soft-faced gates** The idea of a padded gate which can be pushed open by a vehicle, and which then swings back slowly but firmly, to control the speed and frequency of following vehicles, is a possibility, although it has not been introduced on public roads (Fig. 7.23). A very basic version exists in Windsor Great Park, but on the whole local authorities look askance on such schemes because of the problems of vandalism, of liabilities for damages to vehicles and children, of being abused by motorists who try to keep them open, and of cost. However, the idea might be worth pursuing in certain special situations.

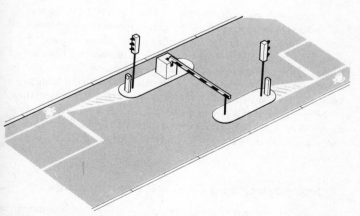

Figure 7.24 Lifting-arm barrier.

(v) **Lifting arm barriers** Although soft-faced gates have not been given a full trial and access ramps have the potential for much development to bring traffic volumes down towards 100 vph, road humps and road narrowings will generally only control volumes down to 1,000 vph. The only other way of controlling vehicle flow to 100 vph, which has been practically tested, is a lifting arm barrier (Fig. 7.24), which can be tuned to allow any vehicle flow required. Furthermore, larger numbers of vehicles can be allowed to pass at peak periods, thus avoiding bad tail-backs without allowing free flow out of peak periods.

However, this method does present a considerable visual intrusion, encourages vandalism, and has a high initial cost. Such a barrier is currently operating successfully in the London Borough of Wandsworth, but no detailed evaluation of it has yet taken place.

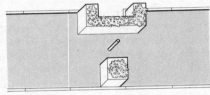

Figure 7.25   An attractive road closure.

Barrier design

The attractiveness of barriers may well be a crucial factor in making road closures acceptable to local residents, though the opposite may apply when residents resent the money spent. However, such costs need not be great; £200 would ensure a minimum of planting and kerbing. In experimental schemes the carriageway must not be altered in any way; one solution might therefore be to put large plant containers directly in the road. If the closure is made permanent these can be grouped together and placed on the pavement of the final scheme (Fig. 7.25). The treatment should reflect the circumstances; more planting of trees near parks, and provision of seats near shops or community centres.

7.6 Signposting and carriageway markings

Informing cyclists that facilities exist is as important as designing the facilities themselves. Clearly, local publicity leaflets and use of the media will play an important part in launching a scheme, but for both local and non-local cyclists careful signposting will be required to assist easy movement of all types of traffic. The conflict which has to be resolved is that of the presentation of understandable information without cluttering up the local environment with unnecessary signposts.

This section describes the currently approved signs and how to apply them effectively for the benefit of cyclists and other road users; explains approved signposting off the highway; and finally, describes the powers that exist for the approval of new signs.

Road signs fall into two categories – direction signs and traffic management signs. Both of these categories can be subdivided into 'Department of Transport signs', approved under the Traffic Signs Regulations 1975, 'suggested signs', and 'other signs'.

Traffic management signs
Only three signs applying to cyclists have been approved:

No cycling (no. 1).[13]
Route available for pedal cyclists only (no. 2).
Advisory route recommended or available for pedal cyclists only (no. 3).

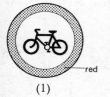 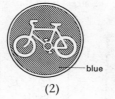 

(1)   (2)   (3)

These signs can be used wherever they are required without permission from the DTp.

A further set of suggested signs are available for cycling facilities after special authorisation by the Regional Controller (Roads and Transportation) of the DTp.

Cycle lanes   The main indicator of a cycle lane is a cycle logo (no. 4) painted on the carriageway with a 150 mm solid white line and blue cycleway signs (nos 5 and 6; see also Fig. 7.26). Contra-flow

[13] See Appendix V for official DTp road sign numbers.

cycle lanes should also be signed with a cycle logo (no. 4) and a white line, unless it is felt necessary to physically separate them from the rest of the carriageway, where a barrier will replace the white line. At the start they should have a separated entrance from the rest of the carriageway with a cycle route sign (no. 2) beside the 'no entry' signs (see Fig. 7.27). Under no circumstances will the DTp permit a cycle

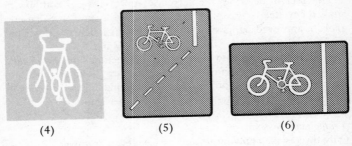

(4)   (5)   (6)

exemption plate under the 'no entry' signs, as it considers that this would lead to abuse of this important sign. A contra-flow cycle lane sign (no. 7) should be used to alert oncoming traffic to watch for cyclists. At any point likely to be crossed by large numbers of pedestrians, there should be a 'cycle lane – look left' sign (no. 8). On side roads approaching the street with the contra-flow cycle lane the

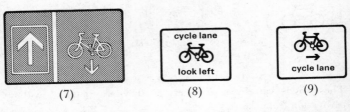

(7)   (8)   (9)

'cycle lane' sign (no. 9) should be used underneath the mandatory turn or restricted turn sign with an exemption plate for cyclists (Fig. 7.27).

Roads prohibited to general traffic   The sign in general use is 'no motor vehicles' (no. 10) with suitable exemption plates (e.g. except buses, except buses and taxis) but the DTp is looking at the possibility of using a positive sign (e.g. no. 11 – buses and cycles only).

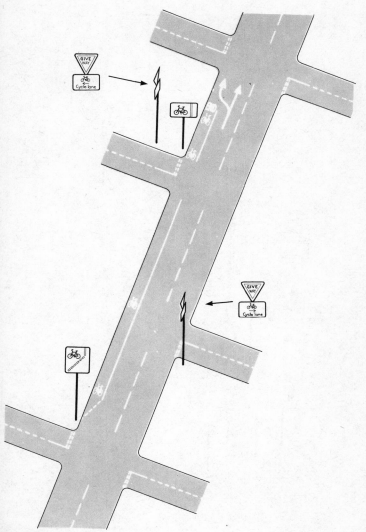

Figure 7.26   Signing a cycle lane.

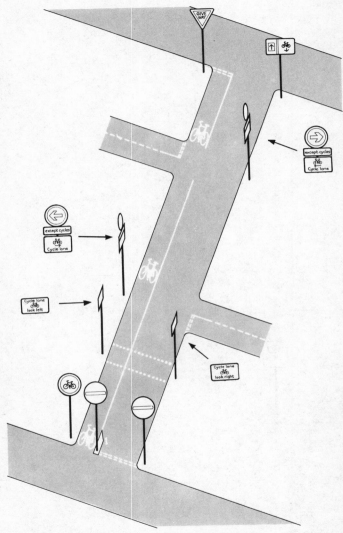

Figure 7.27   Signing a contra-flow cycle lane.

Cycle routes in environmental areas   No specific sign is mandatory to mark a route but the 'route available' sign (no. 3) has been used, with an end plate to terminate the route. The cycle logo (no. 4) has been successfully used in this context and is more useful at minor junctions than the blue plate as it is much more readily seen by cyclists and motorists entering the route.

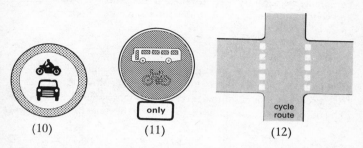

(10)   (11)   (12)

Two situations require consideration. At minor road crossings 'give way' signs should be used throughout, with a newly proposed DTp type of crossing marking on the road (no. 12). This warns motor traffic but does not confer priority on cyclists. Secondly, at a major road crossing the 'beware of cyclists' sign (no. 13) should be used on the major road and 'stop' or 'give way' signs on the cycle route. Where

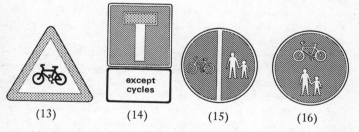

(13)   (14)   (15)   (16)

a road is closed by a barrier the 'no through road' sign, with an 'except cyclists' plate, should be used (no. 14).

Bicycles and footpaths   The DTp current ruling is that all shared facilities must have the sections for cyclists and pedestrians positively separated. Either a kerb or a white line must be used to provide the segregation and the route should be marked with the bicycle logo (no.

4) or cycle route plates (no. 3) at frequent intervals, especially where pedestrians are likely to join the shared route. However, the DTp have recently authorised experimental paths in Peterborough which are shared, but without demarcation. They are currently marked with the advisory sign (no. 3) but in the future the DTp is proposing to use sign no. 15. A special sign (no. 16), which has been in use on the continent, has recently been installed in this country for the first time and will in future be used to denote a separated cycle-pedestrian route.

Direction signing
This is as important as traffic management signing, as it will encourage cyclists who do not know an area to use bicycle facilities. A back street route, for example, may need no more than direction signs to be fairly effective. In addition to marking the route itself, signs will

(17)   (18)   (19)

also be required to direct cyclists onto the route both at the beginning and at intermediate places where cyclists are likely to join the route, and to direct cyclists to their destinations either at intermediate places along the route or at the end.

The DTp does not have approved or suggested direction signs and a number of different types have been used in the past with greater or lesser success, notably the 'cycle route' finger posts in Portsmouth, which did not tell cyclists where they were being directed to, the painted road signs at Balham, which were more visible, and the mini-finger posts at Peterborough, which were informative and easily seen. It is particularly important that a destination is put on the finger post, rather than 'cycle route', which has been frequently used and gives the cyclist no indication of where the route goes (no. 17). It is also important that cyclists get adequate notice of possible movements at junctions without having to dismount. Therefore district names, such as 'Victoria', 'Bedhampton' or even 'City Centre' should be used. Nomenclature such as 'Warwick Road', 'Nightingale Square' or 'High Street', although useful for those who know the area, provides little assistance for strangers passing along the route. A locality should be used even though the cycle route may not go all the way there.

Direction signs can also be combined with the cycle logo painted on the road. In the Balham scheme this took the form of arrows (no. 18) but destinations could be added without much difficulty (no 19). Signs in this position are more easily seen by cyclists than finger posts, which must be high up to avoid being obscured by pedestrians and vehicles.

Signposting off the highway   Cycling is permissible off the highway in a number of different situations (see chapter 4). Signing for these facilities is covered under section 27 of the Countryside Act

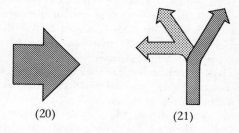

(20)   (21)

1968. Under this Act the highway authority is obliged to sign a bridleway where it leaves a metalled road; the sign must show that the bridleway is a public bridleway, and, 'so far as the highway authority considers convenient and appropriate', the destination of the bridleway and its distance. A later subsection of this part of the act (27/4) obliges the authority 'to erect such signposts as may, in the opinion of the highway authority, be required to assist persons unfamiliar with the locality to follow the course of the . . . bridleway'. The Act allows voluntary groups to put up such signs with the permission of the highway authority.

As intermediate signing is, in effect, discretionary, there are many places where signs would be useful, though they do not exist at present. To combat this the Countryside Commission has produced a standard waymark for footpaths and bridleways. This mark – a signpost without legend – is yellow (BS 08E51) for footpaths and blue (BS 20E51) for bridleways (no. 20). The overall size is 90 mm square.

A junction sign is also recommended (no. 21). It is suggested that the waymark is painted onto a wooden post and that voluntary groups should be encouraged to do this, with stencils provided by the Highway Authority.

Sizes of signs

Just as general road signs are designed to be used and seen by vehicles moving at relatively high speeds, and to be seen despite any traffic obstruction, signs intended for cyclists should also be designed with the speed and position of the cyclist in mind. Thus, of the signs mentioned above only those such as nos 7, 10 and 11 need to be traditionally sized, as they must be clear to motor vehicle drivers. Direction signs and information signs such as nos 2, 3, 5 and 6 should be at cyclists' scale (and no. 8 should be similarly sized and positioned for pedestrians). Already a version of sign no. 2 has been used with an overall diameter of only 150 mm. Signs of such a size will be attended to much more closely by cyclists and will also considerably reduce the impact that road signs have on the environment, particularly in environmental areas.

Attention should be paid not just to the size of the sign, but also to the method of display. One installation has used the small cycle route sign (no. 2) in a bollard; other possibilities would be to place the signs on shorter posts, lower down on lamp posts than usual, and on traffic control gates where these are used. However, signs that stand proud from a post would have to be out of range of blind people.

New signs

A number of the facilities proposed in this chapter present new situations for cyclists, motorists and pedestrians. Consequently, new signs may be required to explain how vehicles should approach these facilities. These signs would fall into the category of signs mentioned at the beginning of this section as 'other signs'. The DTp has the power to approve any signs proposed by a local authority, provided they can be readily understood, would not be misinterpreted, and do not contravene the European Conference of Ministers of Transport rules. Although little use is currently made of this power, the DTp could encourage experimentation with new signs by taking a more favourable approach to the approval of such signs.

In general, the provision of new signs for cycle routes should follow the approach proposed in other sections of this chapter; local

Figure 7.28 'Beware of cyclists'.

authorities should be given flexibility and government should only make firm recommendations after each type has been given a fair trial.

7.7 Bicycle parking facilities

The provisions for parking should be an integral part of any plans for cycle routes and cycle networks. Lack of parking facilities can result in damage to buildings, inconvenience to pedestrians and would restrict the use of even the best-designed cycle routes. Cyclists require places to leave bicycles, preferably in a visible public place, to deter potential theft. Where bicycles are likely to be left for a long time parking places should be under cover.

Legal basis for parking provisions
This is one of the least clearly understood areas of bicycle law, and legal changes are required to make the provision of parking facilities a more straightforward matter.

(i) **General powers** The only authorities to have express powers to provide parking places for cycles are parish councils under s. 46-9,

Road Traffic Regulation Act 1967. Certain conditions are attached to the exercise of these powers – for instance, they may not use any part of the highway without the agreement of the Highway Authority (unless it is a public path), nor may their provision of parking places unreasonably prevent access, or the use of the road by those entitled to use it.[14]

Other local authorities have general powers to provide parking spaces on, or off, the highway under s. 28 and s. 35 of the Road Traffic Regulation Act 1967. The powers are applicable to all 'vehicles', and would normally be used for providing car parks, and setting up metered zones.

(ii) **Cycle racks**   No authority possesses express statutory power to provide cycle racks on the highway. This creates considerable difficulty. Cycle racks erected on the pavement are almost certainly in law an obstruction of the highway. Local authorities must have express statutory powers to erect what would otherwise be an unlawful obstruction; such express powers already exist for the provision of, for example, trees, seats, bus shelters, parking meters, and even drinking fountains. It is possible, however, that there are situations where cycle racks could be positioned on the highway without being an obstruction – for instance, round the side of buildings – but it should be remembered that the law is strict. Also, there may well be cases where it is difficult to tell where the highway ends, and where the forecourt of a shop on the street begins. In such cases, provided agreement was reached with the shop owner, a local authority would probably be safe in providing cycle racks. Clearly, the present situation is unsatisfactory, and local authorities should be given express statutory powers to erect cycle racks.

(iii) **Parking off the highway**   Anyone may provide parking spaces, or racks for cycles, off the highway without the danger of creating obstruction. Employers, public transport operators, local authorities and other organisations can therefore construct parking facilities on their own property, though statutory authorities, and,

---

[14] In exercising their powers, parish councils may:
   (a) adapt land they have already purchased;
   (b) appropriate up to 1/8th of recreation grounds, open spaces, and playing fields they control and manage;
   (c) appropriate any part of a road within their parish, provided the Highway Authority agrees. Such agreement must not be unreasonably withheld.

indeed, companies or associations, must possess the general power to do so. As has been indicated above, local authorities and parish councils already possess such general powers.

(iv) **Individual parking** In the absence of the proper provision of parking spaces for bicycles, individual cyclists tend to lock their bicycles to the nearest lamp-post or railing. No doubt in doing this a cyclist would strictly be creating an obstruction of the highway, but a court would probably not look upon a prosecution kindly, applying the 'de minimis rule' – 'the law is not concerned with trifles'. But if, say, a blind person tripped and was injured by a bicycle parked in front of a shop, the cyclist might well find himself in financial trouble, and his insurance would be unlikely to cover damages arising from what would be an unlawful obstruction.

For the immediate future other local authorities could provide cycle racks either on the highway but in positions where they would not create obstructions, or off the highway, but in the longer term we believe that highway authorities should be given express powers to make these provisions, just as they can provide parking meters and other equally dangerous obstructions. This could be done by amending the Highways Act 1959.

Parking provision

The proper location and type of parking provision is more important for bicycles than for any other class of vehicle since cyclists are generally able to park anywhere, ignoring formal parking stands which are not acceptable. It is fair to say that money spent constructing the wrong type of parking stands in the wrong place is money wasted.

Cyclists, in common with every other vehicle user, want to minimise the distance walked from the vehicle park. The frequency of bicycle parking provision is therefore determined by the extra distance the cyclist is prepared to walk in order to leave his bicycle in a proper rack. This extra distance is a function of the length of stay and the suitability of any alternative parking spots between the final destination and the rack. For example, a cyclist leaving his bicycle for a substantial part of the day, at a railway station or a school, will be prepared to walk further from the bicycle park than will a cyclist visiting a library or shopping. There has been little quantitative research on this problem, but it is reasonable to assume a maximum distance of 75 m and a reasonable distance of 50 m from parking space to destination for long term parking and 30 m to 25 m for short term parking. Clearly, a large number of small bicycle parking facilities will generally be more valuable than a few large stands.

The actual number of bicycle stands to be provided varies widely and must depend on the location and the amount of local bicycle usage. It should be emphasised, from the preceding argument, that a bicycle stand will serve only those destinations within 75 m for long term parking and 35 m for short term parking.

Security

With many bicycles stolen each day[15] security at parking stands is vital. A cyclist should be able to chain both the frame and a wheel of his bicycle to a fixed stand. A bicycle with only one wheel chained to a stand is very easy to steal by removing the bicycle and leaving the wheel. The question of surveillance is becoming increasingly important. Bicycle stands should never be sited in 'out-of-the-way' places, completely unsupervised. Whilst it may be satisfactory to place short term parking stands so that there is some supervision by passing public, long term parking stands should be put in a position where they are always overlooked. In a factory or an office they may be supervised by a caretaker or gatekeeper during the course of their work, and at a railway station by a ticket collector or booking clerk. Perhaps more important than keeping someone on the lookout all the time is to make it quite obvious that the bicycle rack is looked at frequently, thus deterring those who go around dismantling bicycles or cutting padlocks.

Weather protection

Weather protection is an important asset to any bicycle stand, particularly for long term parking, where it should be considered a necessity. The only protection needed is a roof to keep the rain off; 'all-in' enclosures, unless properly supervised, are a disadvantage because they provide cover for thieves dismantling bicycles. The typical roofed bicycle rack is, however, very unsightly and often not particularly stable. When roofing existing bicycle racks or when provision is going to be made near existing buildings, this problem can be overcome by investigating suitable materials: preformed

[15] The Metropolitan Police reports show 15,445 bicycles stolen in London during 1975 and 17,867 during 1976 (i.e. approximately 50 per day).

plastic components or timber structures may prove to be an economical and attractive solution. In new developments bicycle parking facilities should be considered as a part of the whole project so that the shelters form a part of a unified design.

Types of parking stands

The basic requirements for a parking stand are: it should support any type of bicycle without damaging it, either when the bicycle is being parked or when it is accidentally knocked; it should be possible to secure both the bicycle wheel and the frame to the stand; in public places, the stand should not detract from the environment; and an unused stand should not be a danger to pedestrians.

There are four types of parking stands available at present:

single point wheel holders; steel wheel rim holders; concrete wheel rim holders; and frame holders.

(i) **Single point wheel holders** (see Fig. 7.29) This type of holder works by gripping the front (or rear) wheel just at one point on the rim. Security is obtained by chaining the wheel through the jaws of the holder. The holders can easily be grouped together either against a wall or independently. In many ways this is the most successful type of holder available at the moment.

The advantages are:

compact design – cheap to manufacture, almost invisible when not in use;
simple design – no ledges for dirt or water, so a galvanised version is virtually maintenance free with a long life;
single grip on wheel – little possibility of wheel being buckled;
'V' shape – accepts all sizes and shapes of wheel;
single stand viable – adapts itself to oddly shaped spaces and to small groupings.

The disadvantages are:

security – it is only possible to secure the frame if a very long chain is available;
stability – it is possible to knock one cycle into another.

Generally this sort of stand is very good for short term parking.

(ii) **Steel wheel rim holders** (see Fig. 7.30) This type of holder works by holding the rim of the front wheel in a semicircular trough,

**Single point
wheel holder**

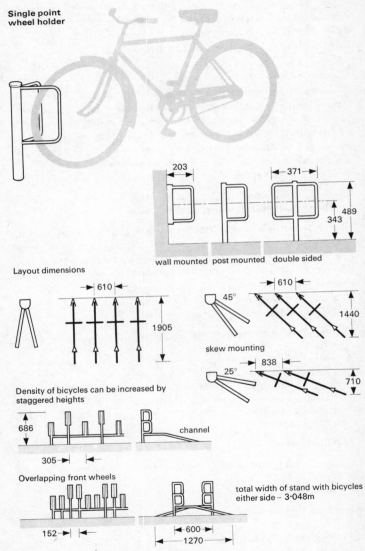

203

371

489
343

wall mounted   post mounted   double sided

Layout dimensions

610

1905

45°

610

1440

skew mounting

25°

838

710

Density of bicycles can be increased by
staggered heights

686

channel

305

Overlapping front wheels

152

600
1270

total width of stand with bicycles
either side – 3·048m

Figure 7.29 Single point wheel holder.

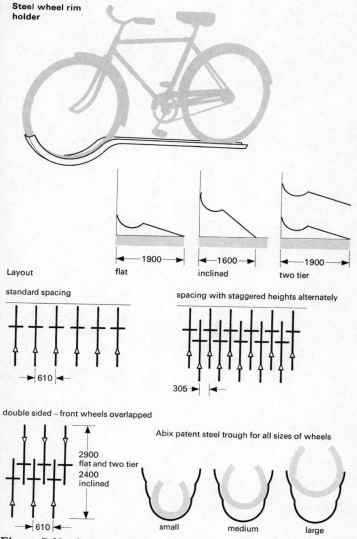

Figure 7.30 Steel wheel rim holders.

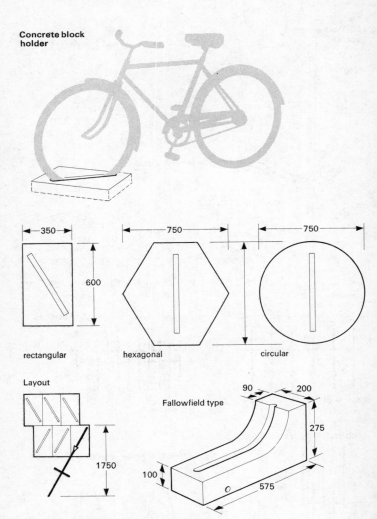

Concrete block holder

350

600

rectangular

750

hexagonal

750

circular

Layout

1750

Fallowfield type

90   200

275

100

575

Figure 7.31 Concrete block holder.

and generally supports the rear wheel also. To cater for all sizes of wheel thickness a complex trough shape is necessary.
The advantages of this type are:

> security – both wheel and frame can be chained to the holder;
> space – with a vertical arrangement the greatest possible density of cycles can be achieved;
> adaptability – all sizes of bicycle can be accommodated.

The disadvantages are:

> appearance – this type is space consuming and unsightly;
> applicability – must be used in groups of six or more; the frame supporting the holders means that the group must be in a straight line.

Generally this variety may be very useful for private parks and long stay parks, especially where demand is large.

(iii) **Concrete wheel rim holders** (see Fig. 7.31)   Concrete wheel rim holders come in the form of grooved precast concrete blocks. The front wheel only is held in the groove.
The advantages are:

> appearance – when set flush with the ground the blocks are almost invisible;
> cost – very cheap.

The disadvantages are:

> damage – wheels can easily be buckled when even slight pressure is applied to them;
> maintenance – the groove must be drained and even then it can become blocked by fallen leaves or other detritus;
> applicability – each size of wheel requires a different block;
> security – it is imposible to secure the bicycle to the holder unless a steel ring is set into the concrete block.

Because of its cheapness this block holder has become very popular. Among cyclists, however, it is the least popular because of its lack of security and the bicycle's high susceptibility to damage.

(iv) **Frame holders** (see Fig. 7.32)   Bicycle parking stands which grip the frame rather than the wheels are becoming more popular. One version, gripping the handlebars, has recently become available in the UK, and is likely to be widely used.

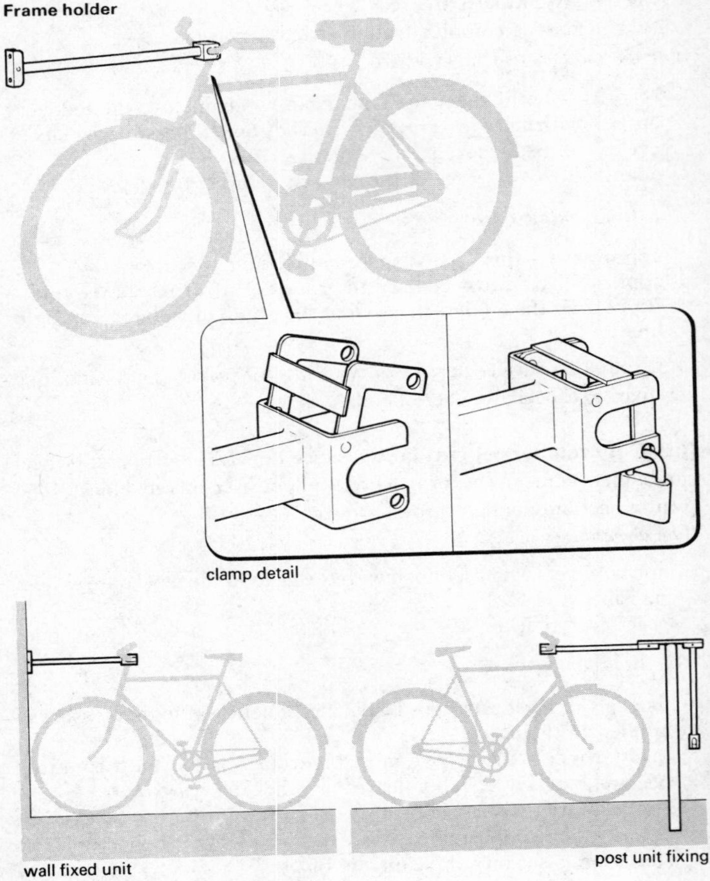

Frame holder

clamp detail

wall fixed unit

post unit fixing

Figure 7.32   Frame holder.

The advantages of this type of stand are:

space – when not in use the stand folds down against the wall;
safety – by gripping the frame there is no danger of damaging the
bicycle;
cost – they are also cheap and easy to install;
design – it will take any size of bicycle;

security – the bicycle is firmly and securely held, and the force on the frame makes it difficult to lift a bicycle up and remove the wheels. However, it does require that cyclists have to use a particular sort of padlock, since ordinary bicycle chains could not be passed through the hole;

applicability – stands can be put in any arrangement and in any awkwardly shaped space.

The disadvantages of this type of stand are:

suitability – it may not fit onto a bicycle which has gadgets attached to the handlebars;

maintenance – the moving parts of this type of holder will require more maintenance than other types of holder.

This type of stand is well suited for both short and long stay parking and if redesigned to accommodate existing bicycle chains would provide one of the most satisfactory parking stands available.

A further type of frame holder is available in the United States and is likely to become available in this country shortly. This is designed to hold the bicycle frame by the rear forks. It can be a hazard to pedestrians when not in use but it does offer the best security of any type of bicycle stand and comes in a number of varieties, including a coin operated version.

Two further types of parking stand should be noted. The 'croquet hoop' type of stand (see Fig. 7.33) combines the advantages of simplicity and adaptability to small sites and all types of bicycle, with

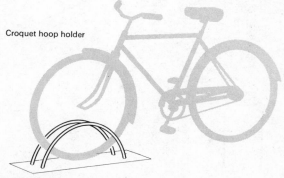

Croquet hoop holder

Figure 7.33   Croquet hoop holder.

stability and minimal damage to bicycles. Generally speaking its advantages and disadvantages are the same as for the single point wheel holder.

The stall type holder (see Fig. 7.34) is derived from the steel wheel rim bicycle holder and has considerable advantages over it – there is no possibility of the bicycle getting damaged and all sizes of bicycle are catered for. It does, however, have the disadvantage of taking up about twice as much room as any other type of bicycle stand.

In general, the ideal bicycle stand is an iron railing and the best stands are those which imitate the function of the railings as closely as possible. Although railings can be used for bicycle stands they are both space consuming and costly.

Where parking facilities are grouped together in large numbers, space is required for manoeuvring bicycles to and from stands. Details of the critical measurements are given in Fig. 7.35.

To summarise, then, properly designed and sited bicycle parking stands are an essential part of encouraging cycling. For provision of security and attractive design the frame holder parking stand is the most suitable design, but it does require a little maintenance. Alternatively, for short term parking the single point wheel holder,

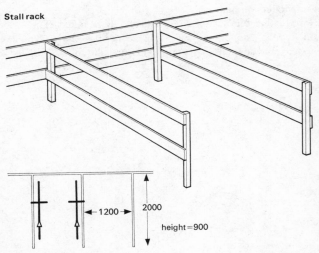

Figure 7.34   Stall rack.

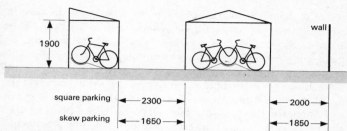

Figure 7.35   Spacing and height requirements for bicycle parking stands.

and for long term parking the steel wheel rim holder, are both acceptable systems.

7.8 Mixing cyclists and pedestrians

We have already shown that in many European countries cyclists and pedestrians share facilities without any serious problems of conflict. In the UK there are many situations where a similar approach could be taken. The best known joint route, in Hyde Park, has been remarkable for the lack of pedestrian and cyclist conflicts.

These conflicts are more likely to occur when:

(i) the width[16] of the route is too narrow for the combined flow-rates of both cyclists and pedestrians;
(ii) either the pedestrian or bicycle flow-rate is disproportionately high in comparison with the other;
(iii) the presence of cyclists on the route is not made clear to the pedestrians or that of the pedestrians to the cyclists.

Most routes which are currently available only to pedestrians could accommodate the levels of cyclist traffic likely to be generated by the provision of joint cycle-pedestrian routes. We believe that every local

---

[16] Few guidelines on width exist at present. For pedestrians alone, widths are normally determined by the equation

$$W = 20F + 600 \text{ (in shopping areas)}$$
$$W = 20F + 450 \text{ (elsewhere)}$$

(W = width in m; F = flow-rate in pedestrians).
(See *Roads in Urban Areas 1966*. HMSO). The width of the cycle route should be added to this as determined by Fig. 7.1.

authority should examine the suitability of *all* pedestrian routes in its area for conversion to joint cycle-pedestrian routes. There will be areas, such as shopping precincts, where cyclists must dismount, but these will be exceptions to the general rule. Similarly, pedestrians may have to be banned on fast, well-used cycle routes.

There is a general guideline which gives a good indication of the need for joint facilities. If cyclists are subjected to a greater danger on the road than they would inflict on pedestrians if they took an alternative joint route, then shared facilities should be provided.[17]

Such shared facilities should be clearly marked with the bicycle signs[18] which would appear at the beginning, the end, and at all junctions on the route. In addition, bicycle logos should be painted on the route at regular intervals to inform pedestrians who join it at

Figure 7.36   Hyde Park cycle route.

intermediate places. Finally, carefully positioned direction signs on the main road should be used to inform cyclists that an alternative route is available.

A few physical alterations to the route may be required. For example, ramps should be provided for cyclists where they have to

[17] This criterion has been adopted by Nottingham County Council.
[18] See Chapter 7.6 for details.

mount a kerb, usually at the beginning and end of the route. These should be gently sloping with a flat surface to minimise damage to bicycles. In addition, if it is anticipated that motor cycles and mopeds may also be tempted to use the route, then bollards should be placed at each end of the route to restrict their entry. This may, however, also prevent prams entering the route.

Where both bicycle and pedestrian flow-rates are likely to be high,[19] some form of road marking will be required to separate the two. Such delineation should be reserved for busy routes or sharp bends and should then be particularly well marked, so that pedestrians quite clearly understand its function and implication. A single white line could divide the route in two, with frequent bicycle logos indicating the side of the line on which cyclists have to ride. In pedestrianised shopping streets two white lines down the middle of the street (again with frequent logos) would give the cyclist a central strip to travel on whilst allowing pedestrians access to shops on both sides. Alternatively, a strip of a different texture or colour could be introduced. If a uniform surface was agreed as a national standard, pedestrians would become familiar with its implications.

There are three basic situations where shared routes should be considered:

(i) **Paths beside roads** These are suitable for conversion to shared paths where they are beside busy inter-urban roads. Here pedestrian flow-rates are likely to be negligible and the paths interrupted only infrequently by driveways and other roads. These would be similar to the original cycle tracks of the 1930s and 1950s, but would cost virtually nothing to provide, so any expenditure could be concentrated on ensuring adequate safety at junctions.

Delineation would not be necessary and in many situations the only work required would be the construction of bicycle ramps and minimal signing. The routes would usually be one-way for cyclists (i.e. in the direction of the traffic) and where bicycle flow-rates were significant and there was only a path on one side of the road, construction of a second might be justifiable.

(ii) **Paths not beside roads** These normally occur in parks, across open spaces or as short cuts on estates. They are often suitable for

[19] For example, we suggest 100 bicycles/hour and 500 pedestrians/hour.

conversion to shared paths, simply by the provision of signs and ramps. Where paths are narrow, or where sightlines are short, delineation may be required.[20]

(iii) **Pedestrianised streets** Many towns in the UK now have pedestrianised city centres. Frequently the roads that were closed were wide 'high streets' which have now been paved over and decorated. Since pedestrian flow-rates are likely to be appreciable in these situations the provision of through routes will not always be possible. However, in many cases a central strip could be marked out by a texture change to provide cyclists with good access to shops.

7.9 Creating complete cycle route networks

Provisions for cyclists should not be random but should aim to connect major traffic generators as directly as possible. Where feasible an uninterrupted sequence of roads with provisions for cyclists, and shared cycle-pedestrian paths, should link residential areas with shopping centres, schools, factories and offices. These routes will involve a combination of the features we have already described; for example, designated cycle routes, cycle lanes and cycle paths. All junctions on the route will have to be carefully examined and, where suitable, bicycle 'traffic lights', sheep pens or provisions for left-turning bicycles might be constructed. Routes should also avoid unnecessary gradients while taking the most direct route available. Even when it is not possible to create a fully sequential cycle route, it is important that as many features as possible should connect with others in order that they are used to full advantage. For example, bicycle 'traffic lights' at a busy junction will be most effective if a cycle lane is introduced allowing cyclists an unimpeded approach to that junction. Similarly, signs off a shared bus lane would direct cyclists into a mixed cycle-pedestrian path across a park, and so on.

All bicycle networks should conform to nationally accepted standards of signing, highway marking and (for some shared cycle-pedestrian routes) surface texturing.

Each design for a cycling facility should be evaluated for maintenance requirements. These may commit an authority to future expenditure which might be unnecessary or to maintenance programmes that cannot be completed, resulting in lower quality routes

[20] See Chapter 7.3 for minimum widths for such paths.

which discourage cycling. For example, a road sweeper should be able to travel along the route; signs should be vandal-proof and highly reflective rather than electrically lit; mud banks which can wash onto the route should be seeded, and removable drainage grids which, when missing, can dismount a cyclist, should be avoided.

To encourage the implementation of complete cycle route networks like these, local authorities will have to adopt new and positive priorities in which the safety and pleasure of pedestrians comes first, cyclists second, public transport third, and the private motor car last of all. Alongside these priorities should come a determination to encourage more people to cycle. With these priorities as the theoretical basis of their transport planning, local authorities should next examine the existing road structure of their towns or cities and prepare detailed plans for modification to that structure.[21]

Long term plans should aim to provide a complete network for a town. Having produced a master plan, priority should be given to improving the most hazardous sections. The order of priorities will vary from area to area; for example, the first priorities might be the provision of alternative routes in parks and improvements at certain junctions. Lower priorities might include surface improvements or the provision of lighting.

These priorities can then be built into an on-going programme of improvements, for which funds should be allocated in the annual Transport Policies and Programmes. Although whole routes might not be completed for a number of years, the resources available would be used to maximum effect.

[21] *The Bicycles Campaign Manual*, which will be published by FOE shortly after this report, has one section describing how to design a cycle route network, which might be useful to planners.

Conclusion

The failure of most local authorities to provide for cycling is a clear cut example of the misallocation of resources which can occur when superficial analysis (of actual movement patterns) combines with professional self-interest (of highway engineers). The basic tools for designing adequate bicycle networks have long been available and there is a considerable body of practical experience in Europe on the application of theoretical principles in practice. What has not been perceived in Britain is the contribution the bicycle could make to the solution of the problem of traffic in towns. The tools have thus been unused.

In response to growing public pressure, central government has now recognised the greater role that the bicycle might play in transport policy. Local authorities have been requested to submit plans for cycling facilities in their 1978-79 Transport Policies and Programmes. This book has been written to assist them with the proper discharge of these new responsibilities. We have surveyed a wide range of practical options available to meet a variety of local circumstances. There can be no further excuse for inaction. The bicycle is a cheap, efficient and environmentally acceptable form of transport. In a time of restricted public expenditure providing for bicycles permits local authorities to distribute the benefits of transport investment more widely and more equitably.

Summary

Chapter 1 Background
The history of cycling is characterised by a period of growth from the early nineteenth century to the middle of the twentieth century. Then, the increased availability of private motor cars and the development of sophisticated road networks, which did not account for the needs of cyclists, signalled the start of its decline. Increasing traffic speed and volume led to greater dangers for cyclists and encouraged them to use other, more attractive, forms of transport. In addition, the introduction of zoned land-use patterns resulted in longer journeys which are less suited to cycling.

The advantages of the bicycle over other means of transport include simplicity, wide availability, energy efficiency, speed in urban areas, and cheapness. These have to be balanced against the disadvantages of the weather, terrain and the susceptibility of bicycles to theft. Although the requirements of cyclists conflict with those of motor traffic, there are many opportunities for partial segregation of these two forms of transport. Only when national and local government policies recognise this, will a significant revival of cycling be possible.

Chapter 2 Bicycle usage
Official statistics underestimate the importance of cycling to personal mobility. The number of journeys made by bicycle, rather than the mileage travelled, should be the measure of this importance. On this basis cycling is seen to be particularly important to non-car-owning households, and to socio-economic groups B, C and D. In some areas cycling plays a major role in the transport system with 10-25 per cent of journeys to work made by bicycle.

The fact that 80 per cent of all journeys are under five miles suggests that the potential for cycling is large. An opinion poll shows that people generally believe that making cycling safer by the provision of facilities is the most appropriate way of increasing bicycle usage. But government transport policy, which is likely to increase the costs of other forms of transport, may inadvertently encourage people to cycle in dangerous and unpleasant conditions.

Chapter 3 Bicycle safety
Official statistics on the relative safety to individuals of using different means of transport overestimate the dangers of cycling. Although cycling is more dangerous than some other means of transport, official statistics mask the fact that it is safer on minor roads and for people over twenty. However, it is other motor vehicles that present dangers to cyclists. They are responsible for twice as many accidents involving bicycles as are cyclists themselves.

The current safety argument, that on a mile per mile basis cycling is ten times as dangerous as driving and therefore that encouraging cycling increases accident rates, is fallacious. This figure represents the dangers that an individual accepts when using a particular means of transport. Public policy, however, should be based on an analysis of the dangers to the whole community, resulting from other people using different forms of transport. This analysis would include the safety of people who do not use motorised forms of transport such as pedestrians and cyclists.

Chapter 4 Bicycle law
Bicycle law is currently confused and contradictory because laws were primarily made to control and cater for other forms of transport. The law makes the provision of cycling facilities difficult and sometimes impossible. Considerable research will be required to determine the most beneficial ways of amending current law. One approach would be to separate bicycles from their categorisation with other vehicles and create laws which give cyclists rights and responsibilities more suited to their particular form of transport.

Chapter 5 The state of bicycle planning abroad
European countries, notably Sweden, Germany and Holland, have provided many facilities for cyclists. Greater concern about bad accident rates and the need for improved inner-city traffic management has resulted in the provision of a range of facilities including shared bicycle-pedestrian paths and improved junction control. Their approach to the problems and their practical solutions give planners and engineers examples which are applicable to the UK.

Chapter 6 Current provision for cycling in the UK

Provisions for cyclists exist in a few new towns and three established towns. In the new towns the networks are often incomplete and inconsistent. In Portsmouth and Balham, the two existing towns which have unsuccessfully introduced experimental networks, the importance of detailed practical and political considerations has been demonstrated. These have, to a certain extent, been incorporated in the networks in Peterborough and Swindon and in plans in Bedford, all of which provide practical examples of the type of cycling facility which we envisage are appropriate to many towns and cities in the UK.

Chapter 7 Designing bicycle facilities

There are a number of ideal conditions for cycling and a number of different types of cycling facility. The standards which apply to the design of cycle facilities need to be flexible to give planners and engineers opportunities for local initiatives. The problems of junction design, of keeping traffic out of designated cycle routes, of signposting and parking facilities and the opportunities for providing shared bicycle-pedestrian facilities are all described within this context. Complete cycle route networks can be created by linking together all these elements. These should be designed to minimise regular maintenance. Having prepared a master-plan, priority should be given to improving the most hazardous sections to ensure that resources are used to maximum effect.

Appendix I

Bibliography

We have included in this bibliography items which relate to the issues which are raised in our report. People who would like further references should obtain a copy of the *Bibliography For Bicycle Transportation* published by the Transport Studies Group, Polytechnic of Central London (35 Marylebone Road, London NW1).

Chapter 1. Background

BICYCLES, CARS AND ENERGY. Eric Hirst. *Traffic Quarterly*, October 1974.

> This article estimates the energy requirements for cycling and the potential energy and financial savings of a shift from car to bicycle travel.

BICYCLE COMMUTING, ITS POTENTIAL FOR REDUCING HIGHWAY AND TRANSIT CONGESTION AND THE IMPLICATIONS FOR TRANSPORTATION PLANNING AGENCIES. D. F. Schula. *Research News*, Vol. 17, No. 2, June 1975.

> Outlines some of the advantages and disadvantages of using the bicycle for commuting in America and looks at the factors involved in the individual's decision to use this form of transport in urban areas.

FITNESS ON 40 MINUTES A WEEK. M. Curruthers. London: Futura, 1976.

THE FUTURE OF THE BICYCLE – ITS PROBLEMS AND POTENTIALITIES. D. G. Wilson. *Long Range Plan*, Vol. 8, No. 2, April 1975.

> Argues that the bicycle will undoubtedly be improved upon but is unlikely to be supplanted as the most energy efficient short-distance form of transport. Whether or not its share of the number

of trips made increases dramatically depends partly on design improvements and partly on the increasing costs and restraints on motor vehicle use, but to a greater extent on the success with which planners solve the highway intersection problem.

GETTING NOWHERE FAST. M. Hamer. London: Friends of the Earth, 1976.

Discusses the implications of current transport policy and looks at an alternative approach based on less movement.

KING OF THE ROAD. Andrew Ritchie, London: Wildwood House, 1975.

A fascinating history of the bicycle from the earliest hobby-horse to the modern racing machines.

PROVISIONS FOR CYCLISTS. Traffic Advisory Unit. London: DOE, 1975.

States the design criteria which the DOE considers should be adopted for bicycle facilities. It is only intended as a guide and is currently being updated.

RESIDENTIAL ROADS AND FOOTPATHS – LAYOUT CONSIDERATIONS. DTp. London: HMSO, 1977.

SIGNING FOR CYCLISTS. DOE. London: HMSO, 1976.

Gives details of the signs that may (or may not) be used.

TRAFFIC IN GENERAL IMPROVEMENT AREAS. DOE. London: HMSO, 1974.

TRANSPORT POLICY – A CONSULTATION DOCUMENT. DOE. London: HMSO, 1976.

Sets out a series of questions on transport policy for public comment.

TRANSPORT POLICY – 1977. DTp. London: HMSO, Cmnd No. 6836, 1977.

Describes current transport policy following the public consultation.

THE WESTERN WAY OF DEATH. M. Curruthers. London: Davis-Poynter, 1974.

Chapter 2.   Bicycle usage

ANNUAL ABSTRACT OF STATISTICS. Central Statistical Office. London: HMSO, 1974.

NATIONAL TRAVEL SURVEY. DTp. London: HMSO, 1975-76.

PEDESTRIAN AND CYCLE JOURNEYS IN ENGLISH URBAN AREAS. London: Transport and Road Research Laboratory, 1973.

TRANSPORT STATISTICS. DOE. London: HMSO, 1974 (published annually).

Chapter 3. Bicycle safety

THE ISSUE OF SAFETY IN PLANNING FOR THE CYCLIST. J. Howe. *The Highway Engineer*, March 1977.

PEDAL CYCLES INVOLVED IN PERSONAL INJURY ACCIDENTS 1972-1975. Greater London Road Safety Unit. March 1977.

PEDAL CYCLIST CASUALTIES IN LONDON. London: Metropolitan Police, B5 Branch, 1975.

ROAD ACCIDENTS IN GREAT BRITAIN. DOE. London: HMSO, 1974 (published annually).

USE AND ABUSE OF ACCIDENT RATES. R. A. Chapman. *The Surveyor*. 16 August 1974.

NOTES ON ROAD ACCIDENT STATISTICS. H. Johnson and G. Garwood. Road Research Laboratory Report, No. LR 394. 1971.

Chapter 5. The state of bicycle planning abroad

BICYCLE PLANNING IN SWEDEN. P. Trevelyan. *Traffic Engineering and Control*, February 1976.

Discusses the role of central government in Sweden to promote cycling in urban areas and gives examples from Stockholm and Västerås.

BICYCLE TRAFFIC IN AMSTERDAM. Town Planning Department, Amsterdam, 1975 (English).

A general description of the current situation in Amsterdam and the objectives of bicycle planning.

CYKELEN I STADSPLANEN (Cycleways in City Planning). Cykel-och Mopedframjandet, Sweden, 1971.

The Transport and Road Research Laboratory have done a translation of this report.

CYKELN (Swedish design manual). Report No. 33, Part I: *Statens Planverk*, 1975.

THE DELFT BIKE-WAY SYSTEM. Openbare Werken, Delft, 1976 (English).

HIGHWAY DESIGN MANUAL. California Department of Transportation, 1974.

INVESTING IN URBAN BICYCLE FACILITIES. R. C. Podolske. *Transportation Engineering Journal*, August 1974.

> Criticises government reaction to the 'bicycle boom' in America, arguing that it is a long-term trend. Greater investment in bicycle facilities is justified in terms of the benefit to physical health, the environment, and because of relatively low costs in comparison with motorised transport.

PLAN FOR BICYCLES IN STOCKHOLM MUNICIPALITY. C. V. Ekman, Stockholm Streets Department, 1975 (English translation by Transport and Road Research Laboratory).

Chapter 6.   Current provisions for cycling in the UK

BICYCLE PLANNING AT THE LOCAL LEVEL: THE LONDON EXPERIENCE. PTRC Conference Proceedings. *Urban Traffic Models*, Vol. II, 1974.

> Examines the extent of bicycle use in London arguing that it has a considerable contribution to make to peak hour work trips by adults and recreation trips by children. It then investigates in detail the effects of road planning since 1945 on the ease of bicycle movement and examines the relevance of modelling techniques in this area.

BICYCLE PLANNING IN LONDON. P. Trevelyan. *The Planner*, Vol. 61, June 1975.

CAMBRIDGE CYCLEWAYS REPORT. Cambridge: City Architect and Planning Office, 1975.

CYCLE ROUTES IN PORTSMOUTH. SR317. Crowthorne: Transport and Road Research Laboratory, 1978.

CYCLING IN NOTTINGHAM. E. Claxton, British Cycling Bureau (unpublished).

CYCLING IN WANDSWORTH. Director of Technical Services. London: Wandsworth Borough Council, 1975.

NEW PROVISIONS FOR CYCLISTS IN MIDDLESBROUGH. B. Smith-Boyes. Polytechnic of Central London, 1976.

NOTES FOR GUIDANCE IN THE PROVISION OF FACILITIES FOR PEDAL CYCLISTS. Greater London Council, 1976.
PROVISIONS FOR CYCLISTS IN THE MEDIUM-SIZED URBAN AREA – BEDFORD. P. Snelson. County Planning Office, 1976.
STEVENAGE CYCLEWAY SYSTEM. Stevenage Development Corporation, 1974.
SWINDON TRANSPORTATION STUDY. Interim Reports. Wiltshire County Council, 1977.

Chapter 7. Designing bicycle facilities

AMENAGEMENTS EN FAVEUR DES CYCLISTES ET CYCLOMOTEURISTES. Setra Division Urbaine, 1975 (English translation by Goulden and Hyman, 1976).
BICYCLES AND PEDESTRIANS. OECD Working Document, 1975.
BICYCLE AND PEDESTRIAN PLANNING AND DESIGN. MAUDEP, PO Box 772, Church Street Station, New York, USA, 1971.
BIKEWAY PLANNING CRITERIA AND GUIDELINES. UCLA, Department of Public Works, Sacramento, USA, 1972.
ON THE RIGHT RACK. M. Pion. STC Environment Club (Harlow), 1976.
PLANNING CRITERIA FOR BIKEWAYS. V. R. Desimone. *Transportation Engineering Journal*, Vol. 99, August 1973.
WAYMARKING. The Countryside Commission. London: HMSO, 1974.

Appendix II

Current progress in the provision of cycling facilities in the UK

This appendix describes cycling facilities which have been provided or are currently planned for towns and cities of the UK. It supplements Chapter 6, which highlighted particular developments which merited detailed description. The figures in brackets after town names give the percentage of journeys to work which are undertaken by bicycle. They give an indication of the importance of cycling in each particular town.

Aberdeen (1·3 per cent)

Cyclists are allowed to use parts of a 5 mile section of disused railway line which the District Council has recently purchased. No special facilities have been provided and the route is discontinuous where bridges have been dismantled.

Basildon (5·2 per cent)

In 1965 the Development Corporation suggested a limited cycle route system linking residential and industrial areas. To date 7 km of the routes have been built and further sections will be added as and when new residential areas are completed. Bicycle parking facilities are available in the neighbourhood centres and in the town centre itself.

Basingstoke (6·4 per cent)

Basingstoke has a few short lengths of cycle tracks. Five subways have segregated facilities for pedestrians and cyclists and there are 100 bicycle parking spaces in the town centre.

Bedford (18·8 per cent)

More bicycles than cars are owned in Bedford. Development of a 36 km bicycle network is proposed, linking areas of employment with residential areas. Part of a disused railway line will be used; two underpasses and two new river bridges are proposed; eighteen new sets of traffic lights are envisaged, specifically to help cyclists and pedestrians. Some footpaths and the river towpath are already used by cyclists. Cycling is to be encouraged by signposting, relaxing local bye-laws in parks, extending existing cycle tracks and providing parking facilities. There is an annual provision of £20,000 in the Transport Policies and Programme for the next five years. Work was due to start in April 1977.

Birmingham (1·3 per cent)

The central area of 1,000 hectare Sutton Park has been designated for use by cyclists and walkers only. There is a cycle track in Aston Park which is used for teaching children cycling proficiency and road safety. There are some bicycle parking facilities at railway stations and cyclists are allowed to use the pedestrianised zones in the city centre.

Bournemouth/Poole (7·6 per cent)

At present, there are no special facilities in either town but the local FOE group has produced proposals[1] for a network of cycle routes and bicycle parking facilities for the area.

Bracknell (30·0 per cent)

Cycling is allowed along main footpaths (as a result of a local bye-law) and these connect with cycleways in the housing estates.

Cambridge (30·0 per cent)

A report was published by the council in 1975 proposing several facilities to help cyclists in the short term. In the longer term a

[1] *Easy Riding.* Feb. 1976. Available from Poole FOE.

network of routes has been suggested for implementation over a fifteen-year period. The short-term ideas which should be introduced before 1981 include the provision of cycle tracks, cycle lanes, signal controlled crossings, island refuges for cyclists, access restrictions favouring cyclists and traffic restraint on certain roads. The original proposals called for an investment of £200,000 on cycling facilities before 1981 but only £10,000 has been spent in the first two years. However, an early start is to be made on implementing the designated cycle routes within the network. A survey of all existing paths used by cyclists is to be completed in order to establish future needs for resurfacing and maintenance. All existing pedestrian bridges over the river are to be checked with a view to adapting them for easier use by cyclists. Existing bicycle parking facilities are to be improved and the council will identify areas where more could be provided. 300 covered parking spaces have been provided at the main railway station. A standard for the provision of bicycle parking spaces in all new developments is to be adopted by the council. However, a change in local government in 1976 has put the future of these plans in jeopardy.

Carlisle (3·4 per cent)

Cyclists are allowed access to the (pedestrianised) city centre area. A bicycle slip path has been built from the inner ring road, leading to the city centre area. Cyclists can use a contra-flow bus lane near the city centre.

Chelmsford (17·7 per cent)

There are two cycle routes totalling 2 miles and bicycle parking facilities at a multi-storey car park in the town centre, as well as at other strategic places. Some of these are under cover. A system of 11 kms (7 miles) of cycle routes has been agreed in principle by the county council for construction as and when finance becomes available. The scheme will link residential areas with the town centre and an industrial zone (New Street). Part of it is already in existence and the rest will be provided by the construction of new footways and cycle routes and the improvement of existing footways for use by cyclists.

Cheltenham (11·3 per cent)

The building of a new bypass gave the council an opportunity to build a bicycle underpass which links a residential development with an employment area. In addition, the council is actively looking at ways to improve facilities for cyclists by allowing them to use bus-only lanes and access roads; by providing more bicycle parking spaces; and by exempting cyclists from street closures.

Craigavon (5·6 per cent)

There is an extensive segregated cycle track system throughout this new town. In parts of the town that have not yet been built, provision has been made for subways under main roads that will be shared by pedestrians and cyclists.

Crewe (23·3 per cent)

Local councillors have suggested that a special cycle route should be provided along the Crewe/Nantwich main road in view of the large number of cyclists already using this route. This is currently awaiting DTp approval. There are already some parking spaces in the town centre, in large factories (e.g. Rolls Royce) and at railway stations.

Daventry (5·7 per cent)

Several underpasses have facilities for cyclists and pedestrians. Planning briefs in future will, where feasible, cater for the needs of cyclists by incorporating cycle routes in the new developments.

East Kilbride (0·3 per cent)

A 'riverside parkway' (approximately $2\frac{1}{2}$ kms long) combining a footpath, a cycle route, a nature trail and a pony trek route received committee approval in 1973. The route will link housing estates with the town centre and the surrounding countryside. Implementation of the plan has been halted due to financial restraints but some minor preparatory work has been done under the Job Creation Programme.

Harlow (8·4 per cent)

The new town was originally designed in the 1950s to have a 25 mile cycle route network. Ten miles have been built to date, but this is, in itself, an incomplete network. All new development will have bicycle provision included.

Ipswich (15·4 per cent)

Cyclists will be allowed to use the ½-mile bus priority route in the town and will be encouraged to use the existing cycle track near Civic College. Other measures include reversing the traffic flow in one street to give cyclists a shorter route to the town centre and providing bicycle parking facilities in different parts of the central area.

Kingston upon Hull (17·7 per cent)

The council has adopted a policy of providing cycle tracks along some disused railways and filled agricultural drains but lack of finance has made it difficult to implement these proposals. However, the council is safeguarding several routes and considerable lengths of these are already available for use by cyclists. In addition, the possibility of providing facilities for cyclists in new development areas and in the city centre is being considered.

Lincoln (14·6 per cent)

The one cycle track here is a 20 mile stretch of disused railway track between Woodhall Spa and Louth.

Liverpool (1·6 per cent)

No facilities for cyclists exist at present. FOE Merseyside has proposed a cycle route to link the university with halls of residence and another to link with the city centre. Liverpool District Council is interested and has put the proposals to the county council, who say they have no staff time available.

London

Camden (0·9 per cent)

Three measures to help cyclists have been adopted: approximately 60 parking spaces have been provided at shops, libraries, tube/rail stations, and firm proposals exist for a further 21 spaces; all future road closures will include access for cyclists by lowering kerbs and leaving gaps in barriers. Cyclists are included in all traffic counts.

Ealing (3·8 per cent)

The GLC has approved the closure of three roads across Ealing Common by grassing them over and leaving a track for cyclists and pedestrians. In addition, the local council has produced a feasibility study for the central Ealing area which will restrain traffic but will allow access for cyclists.

Greater London Council

In 1976 experimental cycle routes were designated by the GLC in thirteen London parks, e.g. Alexandra, Finsbury and Golders Green. These have now been made permanent. In the GLC's TPP for 1978/9 300 bicycle racks will be provided at 30 stations, subject to the agreement of British Rail.

Hammersmith (2·1 per cent)

A council discussion document on cycling includes:

(i) a survey of existing bicycle parking facilities at stations, shops etc.

(ii) plans for a comprehensive network of cycle routes including the use of back-streets 'rat-runs' and contra-flow lanes.

Haringey (1·8 per cent)

The council policy on cycling includes:

(i) providing bicycle parking facilities at council buildings

(ii) encouraging cyclists to use a section of disused railway line

(iii) providing cycle routes on highways and footpaths, depending on financial resources available

(iv) incorporating facilities for cyclists in planning briefs for new residential developments.

(v) including cyclists in all traffic counts.

Kensington (1·3 per cent)
The GLC is investigating proposals for three short-length contra-flow cycle lanes. Five parking racks have been installed in the King's Road area.

Lambeth (1·0 per cent)
The council is committed to providing cyclists' facilities at the planning stage of all new traffic/housing/environmental schemes. It is also committed to providing a trial cycle route and a contra-flow cycle lane. Three traffic management schemes are to be adopted next year and all have provisions for cyclists. In particular, cyclists will be allowed through road closures. At present the council is considering plans to allow cyclists through parks, five of which have already been named.

Lewisham (1·8 per cent)
The council has proposed a 10-15 mile network of suggested cycle routes in the borough. The first $4\frac{1}{2}$ mile route has received approval but has been delayed as a result of change in political power at the GLC. The route runs via parks and back streets from Lewisham through Catford to Beckenham Place Park. It links railway stations, shops and schools. The estimated cost is £53,000. A leaflet has been produced describing the route and this has been distributed locally. In the long term there are plans to designate a cycle route from Blackheath to Lewisham.

Richmond (6·0 per cent)
The council has proposed using the river towpath as a cycle route. The Engineers' Department are working on an experimental low-cost scheme which it is hoped will be acceptable.

Sutton (4·6 per cent)
The council has rejected the local FOE group's proposal for four cycle routes totalling ten miles. The routes would have used back streets to link shopping centres, libraries and swimming pools. Instead, the council has suggested various footpaths which could be used as 'short cuts' by cyclists and one of these is due for early implementation.

Thamesmead
1·6 miles of segregated cycleways have been built. This is part of a 5·6 mile network proposed for completion in the 1980s. In addition to the

50 bicycle parking spaces at Abbey Wood station, a further 225 are proposed at other stations.

Department of the Environment
The DOE has designated four cycle paths in Hyde Park. One runs from Hyde Park Corner, parallel with Park Lane, on a wide footpath which is shared with pedestrians. A white line on the path separates pedestrians and cyclists and the route is indicated by 'bicycle logos' on the tarmac surface. Other routes available to cyclists in Hyde Park run along Rotten Row, Serpentine Road and Albert Memorial Road. There is also a cycle route in Richmond Park.

Maldon (Essex) (8·3 per cent)

There is a proposal to designate an advisory recreational cycle route scheme within the coastal area between Burnham and Maldon, with the possibility of also including bicycle hire facilities. Consultations on the cycle route are at present taking place with many interested groups before the proposals are submitted to the council. Some operational difficulties regarding the bicycle-hire scheme have been identified. Preference is at this stage therefore being given to implementation of the recreational cycle route.

Middlesbrough (4·5 per cent)

An experimental 4·6 mile cycle route was approved by the county council in 1976 and is due for completion by the end of 1977. It will run from a new housing estate in the southern part of the town, along Marton West Beck to Albert Park. The section from the park to the town centre has been scrapped due to the abandonment of a relief road scheme. The route will use some existing lanes and footpaths and some newly-constructed paths. £112,000 has been allocated from the council's budget and the Manpower Services Commission has agreed to contribute an additional £70,000 under its job creation scheme. The route runs adjacent to six schools and when the 0·75 mile east-west extension is opened a further eleven schools will have direct access to the cycle route network. There will be one underpass and the signal-controlled junctions may have a cyclists' phase triggered by loop detectors in the tarmac surface. A cyclists' training school will be operated by the council. Parking facilities will be provided at the town centre, local shopping centres and at some schools. The scheme will be monitored by the county and district councils.

Mildenhall (Suffolk) (11·9 per cent)

Forest Heath District Council has suggested an 'outline' scheme for a circular recreational cycle route near Newmarket totalling 40 miles, which will use lanes and footpaths. The idea has been incorporated within the draft Newmarket plan. Feasibility studies of the proposed route are being carried out before it is put to committee for approval. It is hoped that the East Anglia Tourist Board and the Countryside Commission will help publicise the scheme. The adjoining East Cambridgeshire District Council also has plans for a similar network of routes which are intended to link with the Forest Heath Council Routes.

Milton Keynes

12 miles of segregated cycleway have been built but this does not form a complete network. A comprehensive segregated cycleway (and footpath) system is planned for the area, totalling 93 miles, using existing footpaths and building new tracks. The minimum width will be 3 m to 5 m.

Newcastle (0·9 per cent)

In March 1975, the council proposed six cycle routes totalling 10-12 miles. The council has started construction of one of these routes which consists of a cycle route using shared pavements and an underpass, and runs adjacent to the A1.

Northampton (7·7 per cent)

There is a 500 yd length of shared footpath and cycle route linking a major road junction with a local school.

Norwich (13·3 per cent)

Three separate facilities exist at present:

(i) one short-length cycle track (300-400 yards) adjacent to the university
(ii) a cycle subway under the inner ring road
(iii) cyclists are allowed to use a bus lane, by-passing the one-way system, saving approximately ¾ mile.

Two proposals are in the pipeline:

(i) cycle lanes will be incorporated in a large new residential development
(ii) cyclists will be allowed to use a further bus lane.

Both proposals are definite and will be completed in one to three years. There are parking facilities at the university, shops and schools, and cyclists may be allowed in a new pedestrian precinct. The council has an on-going policy to help cyclists.

Nottingham (2·7 per cent)

Cyclists are allowed to use many city centre roads closed to motor vehicles, sharing most of them with buses.

Oxford (16·7 per cent)

There are 3½ miles of cycle routes in the area, mostly using perimeter roads and including four underpasses. In addition, four miles of bus lanes are available for use by cyclists. In the city centre some junctions are designed to give priority to cyclists. Three-quarters of a mile of new routes are proposed to complete the missing links and nine miles of 'additional suggestions', including use of the river towpaths, have been agreed in principle, subject to the availability of finance and staff.

Peterborough (25·0 per cent)

A 38 mile primary network and 34 miles of local routes were proposed in 1973. This network consists of:

(i) cycle tracks segregated from traffic
(ii) cycle lanes on roads
(iii) cul-de-sacs through which cyclists can pass
(iv) cycle trails leading to the countryside.

It is hoped to complete the network in the 1980s and the estimated cost is £2½ M at 1974 prices. When building the segregated cycle tracks it is intended that, at first, these will be shared by pedestrians. Provision will be made for adding footpaths alongside at a later date and these will be built when the cyclist–pedestrian mix on the cycleways becomes a problem. The route between Bretton and the city centre was completed in June 1977 and at the town centre existing streets have been closed to all through traffic except bicycles. This section includes one of the first contra-flow cycle lanes in the country. Cyclists are segregated from on-coming traffic by a thick white line and bollards have been placed at the entrance and exit of the route to protect cyclists from traffic. The route continues along a purpose-built cycleway which has a footway running parallel to it but marked with a different surface texture. Following this, there is a section of road with cycle lanes on either side, ending in a series of special junctions for cyclists. These are designed to take cyclists across main roads in safety and usually have traffic signals which are operated by loop detectors which mean that the cyclist rarely has to stop. A final section of cycleway and footway follows and connects with the existing cycle routes in the new town. The use of this route will be monitored by the Development Corporation and the Transport and Road Research Laboratory.

Reading (6·7 per cent)

Provision of 65 bicycle parking racks has been approved by the borough council.

Sheffield (0·3 per cent)

Cyclists are allowed to use the existing bus lanes and will be allowed to use the newly proposed bus lanes following the valley routes (suitable for cyclists because of their easy gradients). When the inner ring road is built it is hoped that cyclists will be allowed to use access roads to the centre, together with buses. There are no suggestions for helping cyclists in the Structure Plan or the TPP but the local Friends of the Earth group has suggested a cycle route network, using back streets and bus lanes.

Skelmersdale (1·4 per cent)

All major roads in this new town have subways which incorporate footpaths and cycleways avoiding the main roads and linking housing, employment and shopping areas. At present two residential and two industrial areas have been included in the network and the scheme will be extended as further expansion of the town takes place. The cycleways were originally designed to be segregated from the pedestrian footpaths. Initially, however, due to low bicycle usage, only the cycleway has been constructed and this will be shared with pedestrians. Provision has been made for adding footpaths alongside and these will be built when the cyclist–pedestrian mix on the cycle routes becomes a problem.

Stevenage (7·7 per cent)

23 miles of cycleways with 90 underpasses have been constructed to segregate cyclists from cars. The facility is shared with mopeds and pedestrians and runs alongside main roads, separated by grass verges. In addition, there are a number of cross-town cycle links which were originally country lanes. The existing cycle network is to be extended to include all new development in the town.

Stoke on Trent (1·5 per cent)

An idea here is the use of 'greenways' consisting of ash paths following the routes of disused mineral lines and flattened spoil heaps. There are three main routes: one of 22 miles, one of 10 miles and one of 8 miles. They link local schools and shops. A forthcoming plan for the city centre includes a proposal for a cycle route to link Hanley centre via a park to the polytechnic, the main BR station, Stoke centre and the polytechnic's high-rise flats. It is hoped to continue the cycle route to a municipal golf course planned for the north of the city, and also to a country park on the eastern boundary. This is due for completion in 2-3 years' time.

Swindon (13·2 per cent)

Several cycle tracks have been constructed; cyclists are also allowed to use footpaths as a result of a local bye-law. Rear access roads have been paved and are used (unofficially) by cyclists. A comprehensive system of cycling facilities is planned for the proposed extension of the town and cycleways in new estates will run alongside paths, shared with pedestrians.

Appendix III

Pedal cycle accidents in London

This appendix gives further insights into the problem of pedal cycle accidents. It is reproduced with permission from the Metropolitan Police.

Adult pedal cyclist casualties

Eight out of every ten of the adult cyclists killed or injured during 1974 were males and 29 per cent of the males were in the 15 to 19 age group.

78 per cent of adult pedal cyclist injuries occur during daylight. 93 per cent happen on 30 mph roads. The worst hours for adult cyclist casualties are the peak traffic hours from 8 to 9 am and 5 to 6 pm. More adult cyclists were injured on Friday than on any other day of the week during 1974 and January had the highest monthly total.

The report books for 239 accidents in which adult pedal cyclists were injured during 1974 have been studied and the results were:

(a) *Accident types*

1. Collision with stationary or parked vehicle (13 per cent) – includes 30 cases of 'opening door negligently'.
2. Failure to comply with junction control (12 per cent) – cyclist at fault in only 5 of 29 accidents.
3. Turning injudiciously (12 per cent) – 17 right, 8 left and 3 'U' turns with the cyclist at fault on only 7 occasions.
4. Overtaking injudiciously (7 per cent) – cyclist at fault in 4 out of 16 accidents.
5. Roundabout accidents (6 per cent) – cyclist blameworthy in only 4 of 14 cases.
6. Inattentive or attention diverted (6 per cent) – cyclist at fault in 11 out of 14 accidents.

7. Moving across path of other vehicle (5 per cent) – cyclist at fault in 5 out of 13 accidents.
8. Travelling too close to vehicle in front (5 per cent) – cyclist at fault in 6 out of 12 cases.
9. Cyclist loses balance (4 per cent).
10. Others (30 per cent) – including 6 mechanical faults (5 bicycle defects) and 5 defective road surfaces.

In 18 (8 per cent) of the accidents the pedal cycle was the only vehicle involved, although this includes 5 collisions with pedestrians and one with a dog. The adult cyclists were mainly to blame for 31 per cent of the accidents and other road users were responsible for some 58 per cent. In the remaining 11 per cent of the accidents the blame was shared between both parties involved.

(b) *Road surface and weather conditions*
Only 46 (19 per cent) of the 239 accidents occurred on wet or greasy road surfaces and the weather was other than fine or sunny on only 33 (14 per cent) of the occasions.

(c) *Junctions and type of road*
189 (79 per cent) of the accidents were located at, or within 20 yards of, a junction of some kind. This includes 10 at private drives or entrances. 17 (7 per cent) of the accidents happened on dual carriageways.

(d) *Other road users involved*

	Non-casualties	Casualties	Total	
Car drivers	160	4	164	(70·7%)
Van drivers	26	0	26	(11·2%)
Lorry drivers	9	0	9	(3·9%)
Pedestrians	3	5	8	(3·4%)
Motor cyclists	5	0	5	(2·2%)
Other cyclists	1	0	1	(0·4%)
Others	18	1	19	(8·2%)
	222	10	232	(100·0%)

(e) *Pedal cycle types*
The 242 pedal cycles involved in the 239 accidents includes two tandems, a handbuilt bicycle and a child's bicycle ridden by an

84-year-old man. Five men were riding ladies' cycles and four women were riding gents' bikes.

(f) Injuries to pedal cyclists

In some cases the injuries sustained by the pedal cyclist casualty were very minor and/or not recorded in any detail. 192 (88 per cent) of the 218 injuries which were reported in sufficient detail have been classified and summarised in Fig. AIII.1 (all percentages shown are of the 218 total injuries). The 26 injuries not shown in Fig. AIII.1 are: general bruises (14); bruised legs (6); hand bruises (2); concussion (1); shoulder blade (1); burst varicose vein (1); and an unspecified fracture.

It would appear that pedal cyclists receive an equal proportion (about a third) of their injuries on each side of the body and a further 20 per cent to the head. Only 33 (13·6 per cent) of the 242 pedal cyclist casualties were detained in hospital, 99 (40·9 per cent) were definitely not detained, 75 (31 per cent) declined any medical aid and there were 35 (14·5 per cent) 'not knowns'.

(g) Damage to pedal cycles

The following figures indicate that the 242 cycles involved in the 239 accidents had twice as much damage to the front wheel and forks as to the rear wheel and mudguard.

Front wheel and forks	25·6%
Handlebars, headlamp and front carrier	8·6%
Rear wheel and rear mudguard	12·7%
Brakes, pedals or saddle	4·4%
Both wheels	2·5%
Extensive damage/Write off, etc	2·9%
Slight damage	2·9%
No damage	22·9%
Not known	17·5%
	100·0%

(h) Reporting of accidents

It seems that as many of the accidents were reported by the pedal cyclist as by the other party involved. Only about two-fifths of the accidents were reported at the scene, over a half were reported later at a police station and another 8 per cent at a hospital or elsewhere.

Pedal cyclists injuries

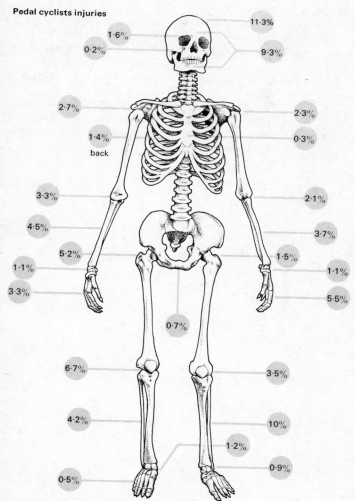

11·3%

1·6%

0·2%

9·3%

2·7%

2·3%

1·4%
back

0·3%

3·3%

2·1%

4·5%

3·7%

5·2%

1·5%

1·1%

1·1%

3·3%

5·5%

0·7%

6·7%

3·5%

4·2%

10%

1·2%

0·5%

0·9%

The marked figures show the percentages of total injuries

Sample size = 192

Figure AIII.1 Pedal cyclist injuries

(i) *Special features*
The 239 accidents included 14 'hit and run' situations.

Strong wind was quoted as a causal factor in 3 cases and 2 drivers claimed that they were dazzled by sunshine. Roadworks featured in 4 accidents.

One cyclist was drunk, one was deaf and dumb, and another was carrying a petrol can.

An American cyclist, when questioned about not having any lights on the bicycle, produced two lights (white to front and red to rear) which could be strapped on to the right arm and leg. These lights are apparently in common use in the USA.

Appendix IV

Trip generation rates

Data on trip rates is particularly useful when new facilities are being planned and when forecasts of possible levels of use are required. However, at present very little information exists on a nationwide basis and many towns have no data at all. We quote below figures which have been obtained for Swindon, Bedford and Stevenage, but it should be noted that the first two towns have a long history of high levels of bicycle use and the third has an excellent cycle route network.

Cycle trip rates

Typical household cycle trip generations in Swindon[1]

Trip purpose	Cycle trip rate (per household)	All-mode trip rate (per household)	Cycle as % of all-mode trip rate
Work	0·41	2·80	15%
Education	0·12	1·18	10%
Other	0·11	2·96	4%
All home-based trips	0·64	6·94	9%

[1] *Swindon Transportation Study – Interim Reports.* Wiltshire County Council, 1976.

Cycle trip rates in Bedford
by age and sex[2]

Age group	Trips per person per day	
	Male	Female
5-14	0·4	0·2
15-24	0·5	0·2
25-34	0·2	0·15
35-44	0·25	0·35
45-54	0·4	0·3
55-64	0·5	0·25
65+	0·35	0·05
Overall	0·35	0·2

Typical secondary school cycle
trip rates in Stevenage[3]

School	No. of cycle trips per pupil
All	0·20
Boys only:	
St Michael's	0·39
Alleynes	0·28
Girls only:	
St Angela's	0·10
Girls	0·20

[2] *Planning for the Cyclist – The Bedford Study.* PTRC, 1976.
[3] *Stevenage Secondary School Cycling Survey.* Stevenage Development Corporation, 1975.

Appendix V

Department of Transport road sign numbers

Sign	Number quoted in this report	Department of Transport number
No cycling	1	624
Bicycles only	2	625
Advisory cycle route	3	815
Bicycle logo	4	WBM 287
Cycle lane beginning	5	WBM 654·1
Cycle lane	6	WBM 812·5
Contra-flow cycle lane	7	WBM 653·1
Warning of cycle lane for pedestrians	8	WBM 810·2
Warning of cycle lane for vehicles	9	WBM 812·4
No motor vehicles	10	619
Buses and bicycles only	11	WBM 267
Bicycle crossing	12	WBM 294
Beware cyclists	13	WBM 291
No through road	14	816
Segregated bicycle and pedestrian route	15	WBM 625·3
Non-segregated bicycle and pedestrian route	16	WBM 625·5

Index